Anonymous

The Tears of Jesus of Nazareth

Anonymous

The Tears of Jesus of Nazareth

ISBN/EAN: 9783743336711

Manufactured in Europe, USA, Canada, Australia, Japa

Cover: Foto ©ninafisch / pixelio.de

Manufactured and distributed by brebook publishing software (www.brebook.com)

Anonymous

The Tears of Jesus of Nazareth

PREFACE.

WHATEVER originality, strictly speaking, this book possesses consists in the arrangement of its subjects, the grouping of its thoughts, the fullness of its treatment, the fitness of its topics to the spiritual wants of humanity, and the directness of its appeals to the conscience and the heart. Jesus of Nazareth is represented in His double character as a Sympathizer with His disciples and a Compassionate Mourner over those who will not hearken to His voice. His weeping beside the grave of Lazarus is taken as a proof and type of the one feeling; His weeping over Jerusalem as a proof and type of the other. The Author believes that the reflections which have arisen in his own mind while considering these two prominent incidents in the Saviour's life, and to which he has given expression in the following pages, may, perhaps, comfort many who are followers of the Redeemer, and lead some who do not now love Him to feel the compassion of His nature and to choose Him as their eternal Friend. Cheered by this hope he sends forth these thoughts into the world.

NEW ORLEANS, October, 1859.

TABLE OF CONTENTS.

PART FIRST.
The Tears at Lazarus' Grave.

1.—Jesus Weeping at Lazarus' Tomb.

PAGE

The Scene at the Grave—Causes of the Saviour's Grief—Others mentioned in the Scriptures as Weeping—Tears of Jesus Nobler than Theirs—Our Redeemer not a Proud Philosopher, but a Man sympathizing with Men—The Saviour's Smiles—The Redeemer no Friend of Asceticism—Value of the Record, "Jesus Wept"—Tears not Unbecoming Man's Dignity,—as Evincing a Tender and Sympathetic Nature—True Tears not Tears of Sentimentalism—The Man that will not Weep a Man unlike Christ—The Mourner may Weep—The Weeper after Jesus shall find Him a Present Saviour.   13

2.—The Sympathetic Tears of Christ.

Sweetness of the Words, "Jesus Wept"—The Son of God in Tears—Not Want made the Saviour Weep; and the Lesson—His Tears not the Tears of Ungratified Ambition; and the Lesson—Man's Tears often Tears of Sin—The Weeping of Jesus prompted by Sympathy—These Tears prove the Redeemer Human no less than Divine—This Thought the Christian's Delight—The Saviour Sympathetic even in Heaven—His Sympathy the Result of His Sufferings as a Man—His Sympathy Perfect and Everlasting—The Redeemer we need,—God enthroned in the form of Glorified Humanity.   39

3.—A Sympathizing Saviour.

PAGE

Christ fitted by Experience to be a Sympathizer—Sympathy of Jesus ever Ready—Sympathy of Jesus All-powerful—A Blessed Record, "Jesus Wept"—Jesus a Sympathizer in our Poverty—Jesus a Sympathizer amid the Frowns of the World—Jesus a Sympathizer in our Temptations—Jesus a Sympathizer when we feel secret Anguish of Heart—Jesus a Sympathizer in our Mourning over the Wayward—Jesus a Sympathizer when Death bereaves us of Relatives or Friends—Jesus a Sympathizer in all our Troubles—This Sympathetic Saviour Faithful amid our Unfaithfulness, and Faithful Forever—The Backslider and the Wavering Christian should Remember His Tears—The Impenitent should Weep in Regret, and Appeal to the Redeemer's Compassion. 59

PART SECOND.
The Tears on Mount Olivet.

1.—Jesus Weeping over Jerusalem.

Jerusalem from Mount Olivet on the Morning of the Triumphal Procession—The Saviour's Pause, and His Lamentation over the Doomed City—Pathetic Grandeur of the Scene—Jesus Wept over Jerusalem on account of her abused Privileges and her Consequent Punishment—The People Foredoomed, yet might have been Blest—Picture of Jerusalem's Happiness and Dignity, had Jesus been received as the Messiah—The Opposite and True Picture—Solemn Tenderness of the Saviour's Plaint—Sorrow of the Redeemer over Jerusalem's Downfall and the Nation's Fate—Their Spiritual Perdition the chief Cause of His Lamentation—The Example of Jesus teaches us to Weep over those of our Neighborhood who obey not God and Christ—Our Duty to Save them by our Tears coupled with Personal Efforts in their Behalf. 83

2.—Teachings of Christ's Sorrowing Tears.

PAGE

The Example of Jesus a Teaching Instrumentality—His Weeping over Jerusalem an Eminent Lesson—The Redeemer's Self-forgetfulness in all His Acts—This Trait beautifully Shown by His Lamentation on Olivet—His Own Griefs Forgotten in Jerusalem's coming Woes—Tears of the Saviour Indicative of His Intense Benevolence—His Love even to His Enemies and Murderers—Lesson of Kindness and Gentle Dealing Taught by His Example—This Benevolence not Confined, but World-wide—Our Benevolence should be as Free and as Large—Tears of Jesus Manifest His Deep Solicitude for Man's Salvation—In this Anxiety we should Share—Why Christians Weep over the Impenitent. 109

3.—The Saviour's Lamentation over Sinners.

The Weeping of Jesus on Olivet a Proof of the Sincerity of His Wish to save the Guilty from Ruin—The People over whom He Wept He had Labored for in Love; and hence His Tears—Consistency of this Grief with the Fact (well known to Jesus) that the Jewish Nation was devoted to Destruction—Repentance would have Saved the People; but, not Repenting, they were Lost by their Own Fault—Invalidity of the Sinner's Excuse that his Fate is Predetermined by God—The Impenitent. Man Self-destroyed—God's Offer of Salvation to all a Sincere Offer—Every Man Invited in Various Ways to Look in Penitence and Faith to Christ for Salvation—Tears of Jesus still Appealing to the Sinner—The Weeping of the Redeemer Manifests the Dreadfulness of the Doom of those who Reject His Love—These Tears Forebode the Sinner's Eternal Destruction—Now is the Time to Seek the Saviour; now, while God has not Hidden the Things that pertain to Man's Peace. . . . 131

4.—The Compassionate Tears of Christ.

PAGE

The Sinner's Unjust Suspicions of the Saviour—Christ's Conduct Proves His Sincerity—The Redemption He Wrought Evidence of His Earnest Compassion—The Sufferings He Underwent for Men Guilty and Condemned—No Stronger Proof of His Sincerity Possible—The Love Displayed in this Work of Redemption—The Saviour Warning by His Tears respecting the Things of Man's Peace—Man Disbelieving and Resisting the Admonition—Danger of Salvation's being Hidden from the Sinner's Eyes—The Day of Mercy Now, but Soon the Night of Despair—The Redeemer would Save, and still Invites by His Spirit—Impenitent Man yet Doubting—Offer of Mercy Made to the Most Guilty—The Offer Made to all Classes—The Clemency of the Redeemer still in Operation—Last Call to Attend to the Things Pertaining to Peace. 147

Part First.

The Tears at Lazarus' Grave.

"Jesus wept."—John xi. 35.

────── Mary, for a moment, ere she looked
Upon the Saviour, stayed her faltering feet,
And straightened her veiled form, and tighter drew
Her clasp upon the folds across her breast;
Then, with a vain strife to control her tears,
She staggered to their midst, and at His feet
Fell prostrate, saying, "Lord, hadst Thou been here,
My brother had not died!"—The Saviour groaned
In spirit, and stooped tenderly, and raised
The mourner from the ground, and, in a voice
Broke in its utterance like her own, He said,
"Where have ye laid him?"—Then the Jews who came,
Following Mary, answered through their tears,
"Lord, come and see!"—But, lo! the mighty heart
That in Gethsemane shed drops of blood,
Taking for us the cup that might not pass—
The heart whose breaking chord upon the cross
Made the earth tremble, and the sun afraid
To look upon His agony—the heart
Of a lost world's Redeemer—overflowed,
Touched by a mourner's sorrow!   "*Jesus wept.*"

N. P. WILLIS.

Weeping at Lazarus' Tomb.

The Scene at the Grave—Causes of the Saviour's Grief—Others Mentioned in the Scriptures as Weeping—Tears of Jesus Nobler than Theirs—Our Redeemer, not a Proud Philosopher, but a Man Sympathizing with Men—The Saviour's Smiles—The Redeemer no Friend of Asceticism—Value of the Record, "Jesus Wept"—Tears not Unbecoming Man's Dignity,—as Evincing a Tender and Sympathetic Nature—True Tears not Tears of Sentimentalism—The Man that will not Weep a Man unlike Christ—The Mourner may Weep—The Weeper after Jesus shall find Him a Present Saviour.

Jesus Weeping at Lazarus' Tomb.

In the village of Bethany, a short distance from Jerusalem, there lived a family that was composed of a brother and two sisters. The Saviour had spent many an hour of friendship beneath their roof; for, as we are told, "Jesus loved Martha, and her sister, and Lazarus." While He was absent in Peræa, "beyond Jordan," however, and not long before His final visit to Jerusalem, wan Disease appeared in the midst of this cherished circle, and threatened to remove its ornament and hope. Lazarus, having sickened, lay at the point of death. The anxious sisters despatched a messenger to the Friend of their brother, imploring Him to hasten to their help. But no help came. So far from responding promptly to their call of distress, the Redeemer "abode two days still in the same place where He was"; and when at length He did commence to return, He knew, and told His disciples, that Lazarus was sleeping the sleep of death. He deferred relief till relief seemed quite impossible,—that He might lay bare to the bereaved family and to the world the depth of His affection, and show forth unto all the power and the glory of the Son of God.

When Jesus arrived at Bethany, Lazarus had been dead four days, and was now lying in the grave. Martha and Mary, hearing that their Friend had come at last, went out, one after the other, to meet Him, and to inform Him that the prop of their house was broken. The sorrow of the one, though deep and bitter, was partially kept in check; but that of the other displayed itself in outbreaking sobs and a torrent of tears. Both, however, looked for comfort from the Teacher whom they had often entertained; and both, it would seem, had a trembling anticipation that even yet, late as He had arrived, He would do something to relieve their distress, and restore them to their former joy. Calm and self-possessed was Martha as she told Jesus of her regret at his untimely absence; but Mary, hurried away by the violence of her grief, could not refrain from throwing herself at His feet, and sobbing aloud, as she said to Him, in the same words which her sister had used,

"Lord, if Thou hadst been here, my brother had not died!"

Those who stood around and witnessed this scene of sorrow, were deeply moved by the grief of the sisters, and could not but join in bewailing their loss. And the heart of the Saviour was also touched. As He looked upon the saddened brow and drooping head of Martha, and upon the form of Mary quivering in anguish before Him, and upon the moistened cheeks of them that mourned in company with the bereaved, the chords of sympathy were struck within His soul, and His eye overflowed with tears. Then there crept a hallowed awe over the feelings of that sorrowing assemblage; and, for the moment, the beating of their hearts was stilled. A solemn silence gathered around them all, for "Jesus wept." The emotions which agitated Him amid that scene of anxious thoughtfulness, could not be quelled. His bosom heaved sigh after sigh; and the drops of tender compassion rolled down His face in a copious stream.

The memory of Lazarus, and the manifested sorrow of his sisters and friends, wrought upon the affectionate nature of the Saviour, as He stood beside the burial-place of the departed, and caused

Him to shed the tears of sympathizing grief. The manly form which He had so often seen in blooming health, was now lying before Him cold and dead; the hand which He had so often clasped in love, was nerveless and stiff; the eye which had so often gazed with rapture into His, was closed and dark; the tongue which had so often welcomed Him as an honored guest, was motionless and dumb. Lazarus was no more; and his departure had brought the shadow of loneliness upon that home which, while he lived, his presence had cheered and comforted with its gladsome light. All this was before the mind of the Redeemer, while His eye and His ear were filled with the sight and the sound of a surrounding anguish that vented itself in groans, and sobs, and tears. No wonder is it, therefore, that He let the drops of sorrow fall.

It may be, too, that the Saviour's thoughts traveled forward to the time, now so near, when He Himself should be stretched, a lacerated corpse, in the tomb; and when, bereft of their stay and comfort, His mother, His brethren, and His disciples should stand and weep beside the place in which He was to lie in the breathlessness and the rigidity of death. The scene which was before Him, and the scene which was pictured forth by His keen foresight into the future, were very sad to look upon, and so " He groaned in spirit, and was troubled" even to the depths of His soul. The fountain of His sympathy was unsealed, and "Jesus wept."

Nor need we think that these precious teardrops shed at Lazarus' grave were poured forth only for them who were lamenting beside his tomb. Jesus perceived not only the coming sufferings of those who were then His disciples, but the sufferings that were to afflict His followers, in one shape or another, during every age ; and He knew that on such occasions they would need His sympathizing aid. He saw that sorrow would try them at times and in places where He could not appear to them in person, and console their aching hearts. Often should they weep ; but He could not be visibly present to wipe their tears away. Often should they sigh ; but He could not come and let them visibly lean their fainting heads upon His breast. Foreseeing all this, He was unable to keep back the tears of grief which sprung forth from His eyes and trickled down His cheeks.

There was a thought enwrapped in these reflections, however, which soothed their sting, and turned the tears that Jesus shed into tears of sorrowing joy. He knew that He should be ever present with those who love Him in the person of that other heavenly Comforter, the Holy Spirit, and thus be able to relieve their every woe; and He knew that, taught by the Spirit, His disciples would call to mind the holy scene at Lazarus' grave, and make the dew-drops of His sympathetic mourning a balm for all their wounds. His grief, therefore, bitter as it was, was not unmixed with pleasure; for it must have made Him glad to remember that myriads of disconsolate believers would hereafter take comfort from the record of His tears, and that they would be made strong under the assurance that, though removed to Heaven, He still ministers by His Spirit to the wants of the bereaved, and imparts to them the fullest consolation and peace.

The Scriptures tell us of many who have wept, —some from disappointment, some from sorrow, some from sympathy, some from repentance, some from joy. Nowhere, however, do they tell us of tears so generous, so pure, so soul-melting, as those of the Saviour when He mourned at the grave of His friend. Hagar wept because she thought herself about to be deprived of her son; Esau wept because he, the first-born, had been supplanted by his younger brother; Hannah wept because her misfortune was cast up to her by her rival as a fault. Job in his wretchedness "poured out tears unto God," until his face was "foul with weeping," and on his eyelids was "the shadow of death"; Abraham wept in sorrow over his departed wife; King Hezekiah wept when he was informed that he was soon to die; the Prophet Elisha wept at the thought of the evil which the Syrian Hazael was to bring upon the land of the Hebrews. Samson's wife shed tears of deceit before her husband; the daughters-in-law of Naomi shed over her tears of regretful affection, when she was about to leave them and return to her native home. Jacob wept when he first saw Rachel; and he wept, in unison with Esau, when he fell on that outraged brother's neck after their long separation; and he wept when he heard that Joseph, his darling son, was dead. This same Joseph could not help weeping aloud when he made himself known in Egypt to his brethren; and Jonathan and David, when they threw themselves into each other's arms, embraced amid a flood of tears. The eyes of Jeremiah became fountains of water as he gazed in bitterness upon the ruins of Jerusalem; the captives of

Babylon "wept" with grief when they "remembered Zion"; and they who had seen the first temple before it was destroyed, "wept with a loud voice," in a transport of joy, when they beheld the foundations of the second temple laid.

And as it was in the times of the Old Testament dispensation, so was it in the days when the New had just begun its course. Peter shed tears of penitence on meeting the mournful glance of the Lord, whom he had thrice denied. The "daughters of Jerusalem" gave way to tears of doleful lamentation, when they saw Jesus walking beneath His cross to the place of crucifixion; and the bereaved disciples threw wide the flood-gates of their sorrow while their Master was lying pale and breathless in the tomb. The widows whom Dorcas had relieved hung over her dead body with outbursts of anguish, and eyes that dripped with dew. Paul preached the Gospel for three long years in Ephesus with a wet cheek and an anxious heart; and the elders of Ephesus, when they parted with him at Miletus, "fell upon his neck, and wept." Finally, the Apostle John "wept much" in his apocalyptic vision, because there was "no man" found "in heaven, nor in earth, neither under the earth," who was "worthy to open and to read the book" which was "sealed with seven seals."

Long as this record of weepers is, it might be made longer; but, after all of them should be brought forward, there would be mentioned not one whose tears were so entirely unselfish as those that Jesus shed at the grave of His departed friend. He wept for the woes of others, and not at all for His own; though even then the shadow of the cross was flinging itself athwart His path. His noble heart beat not in solicitude for His own fate, but only with the warmest throbs of sympathy divine. And most beauteous indeed was the expression of fellow-feeling with man's infirmities then given by the pure and spotless Lamb of God. It came at the time, and it will ever come, with a rare power from Him who is the perfection of all that is excellent in humanity; for it is a sentiment as finely expressed as true, that

"No radiant pearl which crested Fortune wears,
No gem that, sparkling, hangs from Beauty's ears,—
Not the bright stars which Night's blue arch adorn,
Nor rising sun, that gilds the vernal morn,—
Shine with such lustre as the tear that breaks
For others' woe down Virtue's lovely cheeks."

Had we never heard of the Saviour, and were a

stranger to tell us that, many years ago, a Being of His elevated character came into the world to redeem it from the curse of sin by the offering of Himself as an atonement for its guilt, and by the leading of a life of unstained perfection, we should scarcely expect the narrator to describe to us a person who spent His days in familiar intercourse with all classes and conditions of men. We should hardly expect to hear that a Being so illustrious and dignified mingled freely with every rank in society; and that He conversed with all kinds of people, taught them, and entered cordially into their feelings of hope, and sorrow, and joy. Now, whether we should look for it or not, this was precisely what the Saviour did. Coming, as the Son of God, to perform a work too mighty for the highest archangel, and possessed of a glory before which the glory of the seraphim grows pale, He yet exhibited no outward badge of His heavenly origin; He burst not in regal pomp upon the world; and He erected not a throne of earthly splendor before which men were to bow and worship in astounded reverence and wondering awe. Nothing of the kind did He who was by nature and by right the "King of kings and Lord of lords." He appeared as a man of lowliness,—a man sprung from a family in moderate circumstances, and brought up to humble labor from His youth. And when He went forth upon His more public ministry, He showed Himself the same in character and in acts,—associating, not with the influential and the great, but with those who knew but little of monarchs, and courts, and men of noble birth.

Such was the condition Jesus chose to assume; and in this condition it was that He passed a life that was closed by the bringing in of man's redemption. You do not read of His withdrawing Himself, like some haughty philosopher, from society, and compelling those who desired His company to seek Him in some dignified retreat; but you read of His mingling freely with all classes everywhere, and teaching the people, as occasion offered, the lessons of happiness and truth. He met them as a man among men, a friend among friends; and He entered with sympathy into their wants, their hopes, their gladness, and their griefs. From none did He stand aloof; but admitted the despised, the forsaken, the outcast, to His presence, and gave them looks of kindness and words of cheer. To all that sought Him He paid attention,—extending to each the hand of help, and laying open to each a sympathizing heart.

Jesus felt for humanity in every variety of it, and in every condition. Gentle was He, and kind, and compassionate, to all; for, wherever He found a fellow-being, there He found an object of regard, and treated him as a brother beloved. He sympathized with them that were in sorrow, and them that were in joy; but chiefly did He feel for those who were tortured by the ranklings of grief. Hear Him how He says to the weary in soul, "Come unto Me, all ye that labor and are heavy laden, and I will give you rest!" Mark how He comforts the despondency of His disciples; how patiently He instructs their ignorance; how readily He forgives their waywardness; and how He pities them, folds them in His arms, and pillows their head upon His bosom. Observe Him healing the sick, imparting sight to the blind, curing the deaf, giving feet to the lame, feeding the hungry, comforting them that were in sorrow, and showing to men in all their wants and woes that He is their earnest Friend. Note His kindness to the sinful woman who bathed His feet with her tears; and listen to the sweet tones of His forgiving voice, saying to the wife who had proved faithless to her marriage vow, "Neither do *I* condemn thee; go, and sin no more." Hear Him speak to the nobleman of Capernaum who had left his son lying at the point of death, " Go thy way, thy son liveth." See Him touch the bier of the youth who was his widowed mother's support; and mark how at the word of Jesus' power the dead man started up to life. Look at Him as He stood by the grave of Lazarus, and wept; and look at Him as He gazed down from Olivet, and shed the tears of grief over a city which, though He loved it tenderly, Himself had doomed to meet with a speedy destruction from the hands of its foes.

Tradition says that the Saviour was never known to smile; but the tradition is late in its origin, and nothing worth. There can be no doubt that the happiness of others waked up the sense of pleasure in Jesus' soul; and this pleasure could not well do otherwise than show itself upon His countenance in a cheerful, even if it were a fleeting, gleam of joy. The face of the Saviour, we may be sure, was not always overclouded with sadness, though the Gospel Histories have nowhere positively recorded that He was ever seen to smile. Rays of sunshine must have played around His head; but these, no doubt, were fitful and few. How could it be otherwise, when there was a burden ever pressing on His heart which forced Him to dwell upon coming scenes of mournfulness and distress? Gethsemane, and Golgotha, and the garden of the tomb, kept looming up before Him; and it would have been strange indeed had not the cloud of anxiety which hung over His soul often cast its dark shadow upon His brow. Knowing what anguish awaited Him, He pondered on the thought until it wrote itself upon His face, and even infused a tinge of melancholy into His voice. His, then, must ever have been a calm and dignified joy; and we may well imagine that His very smiles partook of the complexion of His mind. They were sadly gladsome smiles; and, when seen to play for a moment around His mouth, they revealed an earnest absorption of soul that would harmonize with cheerfulness, but not with ill-timed merriment and riotous delight.

Jesus did not refuse the sanction of His presence at the festivities of the marriage in Cana of Galilee; and hence we may consider it proven that He frowned not upon any recreation which, while it was timely, was also suitable to the dignified nature and noble destiny of man. Approving thus of innocent and worthy enjoyment, He was often gratified, we may presume, in looking on the happiness of His friends; and, therefore, we may take it for granted that He gave them, when it was proper, an encouraging smile. That He ever went beyond a smile,—that He indulged in that laughter which in mere man has its time and its place,—we can not easily believe; for laughter seems ill suited to a character so grand and solemn as His and a nature so exquisitely sensitive and so divinely serene. His thoughts were too pensive to harmonize with such an expression of gayety; and His work was too dignified to admit of His giving way to such an exhibition of careless mirth. We are willing to think, then, that the Redeemer never laughed, even amid the most cheerful scenes of His life; but we do not, we can not, think that He never smiled. Smile He did, we firmly believe; and to him that saw it His smile must have been as sunshine to the soul.

No record was needed to tell us that the Saviour smiled; and consequently it has not been told. We do need a record, however, to inform us that "Jesus *wept*"; for in this way we are taught that He who promises to heal our infirmities has a fellow-feeling with us in our sufferings, can enter into our griefs when we mourn, can appreciate our anxieties, and, whatever be our trouble, can bid His tears to flow with ours. We want to know that the Saviour who is offered to us can understand and sympathize with the anguish of an aching heart; we want to know whether He will feel for us in our trials, and be ready to administer the cordial of relief. All this the record lets us know when it tells us in its sweet simplicity that " Jesus wept."

There are those who think that tears are unbecoming the dignity of man, and would allow to woman alone the privilege of weeping when the heart is sad. Time was, perhaps, when some of us so thought, and when we would resolutely check the rising tear and keep it locked up within the font of grief. But we have learned, I hope, that we were wrong; and we now feel that the eye which is never dimmed by a tear is not more unnatural and repulsive than the face which is never lighted with a smile. To weep is human. Jesus wept; and what He did any man may do. If He disdained not to exhibit this proof of tender-heartedness, and to open wide before His friends the fountain of His sorrow, none of us, however stern, need be ashamed to let the dewdrops of sympathizing affection fall. "There is a sacredness in tears." Take them away, and where can you find the suitable expression for grief, for regret, for love ? Take them away, and man would be no longer man. Oh, then, think not harshly of those that weep; for weeping is too eloquent and too solemn a thing to be mocked or despised.

Tears manifest a tender and sympathetic nature ; and this, as abundant examples prove, may well consist with the highest nobility of soul. Consider the grandness of the characters of many of them who are represented in the Scriptures as giving way to tears. And, going out of the Bible, remember how Homer speaks of the sagacious Ulysses as weeping profusely, and represents Achilles,—the poets' model of magnanimity and courage,—as sobbing often like a very child. And the bard, in thus depicting these Grecian heroes, is strictly true to the dictates of propriety, and is upheld by the example of subsequent writers who have described the characters and doings of other celebrated men of ancient and of modern times. Feeling it is that distinguishes man from the brute; and they who will always shut down the floodgates of grief, do violence to their natural emotions, and make their hearts as callous as the flinty rock. There is a beauty in tears, an awful beauty, which, when we see them gushing forth in their crystal streams, moves us with the power of an eloquence that we can not resist. It is pride, then, not philosophy, that forbids us to weep ; and he who follows its behest, will strip himself of his chief ornament, and mar the fair proportions of his manhood. That, we may be sure, is a false dignity which would make us apathetic, and freeze the current of feeling that flows within our breast. It does violence to our nature ; it widens the distance between us and Him who is the only perfect man ; it degrades us from our true position, and makes us yet more unlike our God.

I am not pleading for that weak and pitiful sentimentalism which often manifests itself by tears. The weeping that is noble is not the weeping of self-indulgence; for such weeping has no regard to man's moral culture and to the development of his religious nature. Weeping of this kind can serve no good purpose ; but will only unhinge our mental and moral faculties, derange the working of our souls, and unfit us for the stern activities of life. It can never minister to our spiritual growth ; but will be sure to weaken our powers, to give a wrong direction to our impulses, and to disqualify us wholly for the discharge of our duties to ourselves, to our fellow-men, and to our God. Away with the tears of a barren and hard-hearted sentimentalism,—tears of hypocrisy, unshed over real necessities, but poured out like water over imaginary evils and over the figments of the novelist's brain. Talk not to me of tears like those of the executioner of Paris, who, after he had plied the guillotine all day, was found at night with bloody hands but tearful face weeping over the fictitious "Sorrows of Werter." These were the tears of a wretch, and not of a man. Give me true tears,—the tears of meek endurance, of genuine sympathy, of penitential sorrow, of responsive love. These are noble, manly tears. While they melt the heart, they strengthen the mind, chasten the affections, give a right determination to the will, and improve all in us that is godlike and grand. Such, and such alone, is the weeping for which I plead; for this is the weeping of a wholesome discipline by which the soul is made to exercise its best and highest functions, and the whole man is reconstructed after the likeness of Christ.

From what has been said we learn how great a mistake it is to suppose that every indulgence of emotion is a mark of weakness. Rather is it frequently a mark of power. Man was made to feel;

and it is often right that what he feels should find expression. This is love; and we should never forget that God is love. Who has not known families in which much of happiness is thrown away, because the warm kindlings of the soul are purposely smothered? We can not but grieve when we see the sternness of the father, or the artificiality of the mother, crushing out the embers of affection from the children's young hearts, and training them up in the formalities of an intercourse that prides itself upon restraining all outward show of its emotions. True it is that beneath this cold exterior there are sometimes heard the throbbings of a heart that is warm with love; but, then, that love is almost lost which does not find expression,—lost to him who feels it, and lost to him on whom it is bestowed.

Too often, however, education and habit will make the outward and the inward correspond; and then the fount of feeling, frozen hard and fast, can not be unsealed, and its waters be persuaded to flow. Thus will these children be robbed of their birth-right for ever. Better would it have been for their parents to have burnt out their eyes even, than so to have dried up the streams of sympathy that were eager to gush from their hearts. Oh, the capacity to love is a treasure which can not be too sacredly guarded; and the power to express that love is a power which should be cultivated to perfection. Man was made to love; and it is but right that he should manifest his affection in the family circle, in the social gathering, and in his intercourse with the world. Why should he be ashamed of that which proves his likeness to the Saviour? Man is a sympathetic being. Then let him not withhold the word of kindness, the look of compassion, the tear of responsive grief. Not in vain shall he show to others how he feels for them; for his heart of sympathy shall be like a spring of pure water that pours from the mountain side,—sparkling with gladness itself, and bearing to every sterile field the treasures of fertilizing joy.

Think it not unmanly, then, O mourner, if thy soul is melted at times by sorrow. Give thy feelings vent; and if the tears *will* flow, let them flow unchecked. "Jesus wept"; and thou mayst weep. Thou art not disgraced by weeping, if thy trouble be deep enough for tears. When thou art bowed down in spirit, thou needest not imprison the drops of thine anguish. There is no sin in weeping; only be careful not to murmur in giving way to grief. Though "Jesus wept," He uttered no complaint, but resigned Himself in meek submission to His Father's will. So do thou, afflicted mourner. Weep; it is thy privilege : weep, but never repine. Weep, not in sorrow, but rather in joy; for thou hast no cause to be comfortless, when thou knowest full well that He who wept for thee on earth will soon uplift thee to Heaven, and wipe thine every tear away. Yes, " there is a calm for those who weep"; and that calm thou shalt enjoy forever in the land which troubles and trials can not invade. The Saviour beholds the gushings of thy misery, and He pities thee in His heart of hearts. He does not forbid thee to weep, for He remembers the drops of grief He shed Himself; but He does forbid thee, who art a Christian, to weep like one who will not acknowledge that all the acts of God are merciful and right. Even in thine hour of keenest anguish, therefore, raise thy dewy eye to Heaven in serenest resignation; and, whilst the gentle sigh is heaved, and the pensive tear is shed, confess the justice and the goodness of Him who rules on high. Weep, if thou wilt; but forget not that thy affliction, be it what it may, was sent to chasten thy spirit, and to fit it for that abode which is prepared for thee in the realms of bliss. The Lord would loosen thy hold on earth, and make thee fix thine affections above. Then, "traveller in the vale of tears", be glad in the thought that thy mourning, bitter as it is now, is only the short-lived storm that ushers in an everlasting calm. There is no weeping in the Heaven for which thy soul is ripening under its present grand discipline of sorrow; for there thou shalt hear nothing, and feel nothing, more of grief, but, supremely happy in the Redeemer's presence, and supremely glorious, thou shalt shine eternally " a star of day."

It may be that some one of you is weeping every day in secret; and weeping because you feel that Jesus has not yet become your sympathizing Saviour and Friend. You are sighing over your now discovered sinfulness, and are groaning under the now felt burden of your guilt and the now realized curse of a violated Law. When you are alone by day, the tears start forth unbidden from your eyes; and often at night you feel them welling up from the fountain of sorrow, and bedewing the pillow on which you lie. Troubled is your soul; for you see a just God arrayed before you, and threatening to destroy you in His ire ; and you see an Eternity of misery and despair. No wonder you weep. You ought to weep,—to weep bitterly at the remembrance of your guilty misdoings, and your guilty neglect of God, and your guilty rejection of Christ. Weep, then; but weep not as one who has no hope. You are not yet beyond the reach of help; for the same Jesus that "had compassion on" the widow of Nain, and said to her in her sorrow, "Weep not," is now willing to have mercy upon *you*, and to bid you dry up your tears. Pour out your wants before Him; confess your sins, and beg Him to smile upon and cheer your drooping heart.

Weep the tears of humble grief,—a grief that bows at the Saviour's feet : oh, weep the

> " Blest tears of soul-felt penitence,—
> In whose benign, redeeming flow
> Is felt the first, the only sense
> Of guiltless joy that guilt can know."

Pour forth the tears of sincerity and earnestness : then will Jesus quench your weeping, and give you "everlasting consolation and good hope" in His sympathetic love and saving power.

The Tears of Sympathy.

Sweetness of the Words, "Jesus Wept"—The Son of God in Tears—Not Want made the Saviour Weep; and the Lesson—His Tears not the Tears of Ungratified Ambition; and the Lesson—Man's Tears often Tears of Sin—The Weeping of Jesus Prompted by Sympathy—These Tears prove the Redeemer Human no less than Divine—This Thought the Christian's Delight—The Saviour Sympathetic even in Heaven—His Sympathy the Result of His Sufferings as a Man—His Sympathy Perfect and Everlasting—The Redeemer we Need,—God Enthroned in the Form of Glorified Humanity.

The Sympathetic Tears of Christ.

"JESUS WEPT." It is the shortest and the sweetest verse in the Bible; for He that is spoken of as shedding these dew-drops of compassion is the unchangeable God who has promised to wipe all tears from off all faces. There is no expression so touching, none so soul-comforting, in all the literature of earth; and there are few others that can compare with it even in the literature which comes to us from above. It is the shortest verse in the Scriptures; but rather than lose it, short as it is, we would consent to the tearing out of whole chapters which speak less consolation to the grief-stricken heart. This record of the outstreaming tears of the Saviour lays bare to us the innermost feelings of His soul, and shows us what a deep and exhaustless fount of love wells up within His breast. It tells us, what we long to "know assuredly", that the Redeemer in whom we believe, and whom we worship, is alive to all the sorrows of humanity,—that He is "touched with the feeling of our infirmities", and has a warm and tender sympathy with our grief. Brief as the sentence is, it is full of comfort for every mourner,—whispering peace to the tumult of his anxious heart, and quieting all the throbbings of his woe.

Surely, it is a strange and sorrowful spectacle—the Son of God in tears! This is He who is able to bow the heavens, who can tear up the deep foundations of the earth, and who can smite into nothingness the islands of the sea. But, lo! He weeps. Drops of grief are bursting from the eyes of Him whose every look is gentleness, and are trickling in mournfulness down His pallid cheeks. But wherefore does this mighty Being weep; and wherefore does He sigh? There is a reason why He feels; and there is a reason why He thus exhibits the emotions which are working in His soul.

The Saviour did not weep for *want*, as many have. True it is that, though there dwelt in Him "the fullness of the Godhead", and though He was the absolute owner of the universe, He often, in the days of His humiliation, had not where to lay His head. Frequently was He hungry, frequently was He thirsty, and frequently was He ready to sink under the fatigue of His labors. But never did He shed a tear on these accounts. Throughout the entire day would He travel along the sultry road, having no thought of complaint; and then would He spend the night on the chill mountain-top in the offering of glad thanksgiving and humble petition to God. Rich beyond our conception, He lived in poverty; and, whether as a youth or as a man, He murmured not, but was ever cheerfully busied with the work His Father had bidden Him to do.

Think of this, you that feel the pinchings of want, real or imaginary; and remember that your Lord, though poorer than ye, not only suffered no complaint to escape His lips, but permitted none even to rise in His heart. You may deem your lot a hard one, and be tempted to repine. Looking around you in your daily walk, or lying upon your couch at night, you may cherish thoughts of bitterness, while there is passing before you the affluence of others, and may allow the tear of envy to start up and flow. Thoughtless complainers, ye ought to know that this is not only folly but also sin. Jesus never grieved over His poverty, or because others made more show than did He in the pageantry of the world. Think on Him, the unrepining outcast, before ever you envy the position of any fellow-mortal again; and learn to check the beginnings of murmuring as they spring up in your soul.

Neither were the tears which Jesus shed the tears of *ungratified ambition*. He might have been the grandest monarch the world ever saw; but this was far from His desire. Though "King of kings" in His native dignity, and though appointed, as the divine Mediator, to exaltation at the right hand of the Majesty on high, He lived among men a life of abasement. The honors which the multitude wished to confer upon Him, He refused to receive; and when, in spite of His intimations of the spiritual nature of His reign, they were determined to make Him an earthly monarch, He hid Himself from their sight. To carry out the intentions of His Heavenly Father,—to teach and to redeem fallen humanity,—this was His sole ambition. It was for this that He took upon Himself the form and the nature of man, "humbled Himself, and became obedient unto death, even the death of the cross." Such was the object of His mission to the Hebrew nation, and to the world. That His own countrymen rejected Him, as they certainly did; that they derided Him;

that they mocked Him; that they treated Him with cruel insults,—all this, while it pained His heart, and sometimes made Him weep in sorrow over their doom, never caused the tear of disappointed self-seeking, or of mortified pride, to glisten in His eye. These were feelings of which Jesus had no experience; for He, the gentle and the pure, knew no sin, and was superior to all guile.

Would that this, which is wholly true of Jesus, could be said with even an approach to truth of any one of us who profess to be His disciples and the followers of His example. Too often do we place our affections on some earthly object, and, having clung to it with a fervor which ill befits the Christian, give way to sorrow, when it is taken from us by God's righteous judgment, and shed over it the tears of an unholy regret. Too often do we chase some earthly phantom with all the eagerness of the infatuated worldling, and then, after we see that it has eluded us, sit down and weep with disappointment. Too often do we aim at the honors which are conferred by men, and, when we fail to attain them, mourn over our misfortune with tears, and murmur because our merit has not met, as we think, with its deserved reward. Unworthy weeping is the whole of this indeed;

and how utterly unlike the weeping of the Saviour. Foolish are we, and sinful, to let any of these things stir up the fountains of our grief; for what, after all, are the best affections of earth, and the sweetest enjoyments of earth, and the noblest dignities of earth, to those who are told that they should seek, not earthly treasures, but a crown of celestial glory which shall never fade away?

There are none of us, however perfectly we may have succeeded in steeling ourselves into stoic fortitude, who have not often wept; for the world in which we live we have all found to be a "vale of tears." But, alas! how frequently have the tears we shed been tears of sin! Some cause too trifling to be mentioned has excited us, and made us weep, when it would have been more becoming in us to have borne the annoyance in silence, and hidden it from the knowledge of our friends. Disappointed selfishness has too often let itself be seen in tears of murmuring, and heard in the loud lamentation of complaint. Verily, we are all guilty in this matter. Tears of mortified pride have we poured forth in sinful abundance, and tears of vanity justly rebuked, and tears of anger unrighteously displayed, and tears of ungrateful discontent with the dealings of the God who hath

TEARS OF CHRIST. 45

arranged all things so wisely and administered them so well. It was wrong in us to weep on these accounts; and therefore it was that we did not receive on such occasions the sympathy of our exalted Saviour and Friend. Had we only wept the tears of anguish, of penitence, or of sorrow, He would have felt for us in the time of our distress, and would have said to the wild beatings of our hearts, " Be still!" Then should we have discovered that Jesus did not learn to weep in vain; for, the moment He spoke to our perturbed spirits, they would have been sweetly lulled to rest.

Jesus of Nazareth stood by the tomb of Lazarus, and wept, not from a feeling of want, not from the regrets of ungratified ambition, but *from the promptings of the divine sympathy which beat in His heart.* He saw the anguish of the bereaved sisters, He saw the grief of the by-standers, He saw, perhaps, the future sufferings of the disciples of His love; and, as He looked upon it all, the chord of compassion in His breast was touched, and " Jesus wept."

The tears which the Saviour shed beside the grave of Lazarus, and in the presence of Lazarus' friends, were tears of fellow-feeling; and we ought to be thankful that the Evangelist John has preserved their memory in the sacred record which he has penned. The drops of sympathetic tenderness that fell by Lazarus' tomb prove that Christ was man as well as God ; for they show that He was moved by human affections, as are we, that He entered into human suffering, that He was sensitive to every cry of human woe. When we see Him weeping beside the corpse of His friend, and weeping because the spirits of those He loved were overwhelmed with grief, we feel that He is indeed a man, and that He can sympathize with all the feelings and all the weaknesses of man. Looking upon Him as He rebukes the winds and they obey His voice, we shrink away from Him under the consciousness that we are sinners, and are afraid that He can not be human, but only divine; looking upon Him as He calls the dead to life, we are sure that He is not a mortal, but only an incarnation of Jehovah ; but looking upon Him as He sheds the tear of sympathy before the tomb of Lazarus, we are convinced that, even though truly God, He must likewise be truly man. Then are we made certain that we can share in His sympathy ; and we feel assured that He will manifest a tender interest in our sorrows, will wipe the drops of anguish from off our cheek, and still the fearful tumult of our soul.

Aye, blessed be the record which shows so tenderly that Jesus of Nazareth was truly man as well as truly God. Being thus human no less than divine, the Redeemer possessed human feelings just as we possess them,—though in Him they were refined and elevated by His higher nature, and by His perfect purity and holiness of life ; He felt human want ; He was subject to human infirmities ; and in all points did He resemble His brethren, save only that He knew no sin. Led away by the contemplation of His excellence and power as God, we are too prone to forget that the Saviour, while He dwelt on earth, had all the feelings of a man ; and that even now, exalted and glorified as He is, He has still the heart and the sympathies of a man. It is this human sympathy of His which makes Jesus so lovely in the Christian's estimation, and gives Him so strong a hold upon the Christian's soul. The believer is rejoiced, it is true, to think that Christ is an all-sufficient Redeemer by virtue of the shedding of His atoning blood ; but he feels that something else is needed besides pardon to fit him for the inheritance that is promised to the saints. He perceives that he needs protection from evil, that he needs comfort amid tribulation, that he needs the sympathetic treatment which will sanctify him in heart and life. Knowing all this, and observing how he is beset with calamity on every side, how grief looks grim upon him in a thousand shapes, and how trouble waits for him at every turn in his pilgrimage, the spirit of the believer bounds within him in gladness, when he calls to mind amid his thoughtful anxiety that Jesus is not only his all-sufficient Redeemer, but his Comforter in every time of ill; and that, as a Heavenly Priest and Mediator, Jesus has a heart that is touched by human suffering and throbs in sympathy with every human woe.

The Saviour has gone up, crowned with blessing and honor, into Heaven; and there He is still "God manifest in the flesh", but God in flesh that is etherialized and glorified. In Him we behold the invisible Jehovah made visible in the form of a perfect humanity ; and the splendor which streams from His countenance the eye of Faith can gaze upon (which it could not upon the shinings of God's immediate glory) without being struck with blindness and the tremblings of dread. He is the temple of Heaven,—its ever-shining light; and He towers up therein in all the loftiness of His grandeur, pouring down a more lustrous effulgence than does the angel that is fabled to stand bedecked with brilliancy in the midst of the sun. He is the Lamb seated on Heaven's throne,—the only medium of communication betwixt short-sighted man and the unseen God. Towards Him go forth our affections and our desires; and they centre in Him as the most perfect manifestation of Deity which we with our present limited capacities can understand and know.

Though He has ascended from the scene of His humiliation to that of His glory, and though the human body which He carried with Him has undergone some mysterious spiritual change, Jesus has lost none of the warm and tender sympathy which He manifested while He dwelt on earth. He has even now the same melting eye, the same outstretched arm, the same compassionate heart. Not yet has He forgotten the days of His own "strong crying and tears"; nor has He forgotten the sufferings of His flesh, the taste of "the wormwood and the gall." Still is He with His afflicted people; and He has put at their command all the resources of His power and His love. Does their faith grow weak? He strengthens it. Does their affection begin to languish? He revives it. Does trouble fall upon them? He sanctifies it to their spiritual good. Does sorrow come? He administers to them the needed consolation. In Him, their great High Priest, they know themselves to be complete; for He gives them wisdom to guide their steps aright, and fortitude to endure their trials; and, making them holy, He fits them for eternal bliss.

It is a fact fraught with comfort to all His disciples that Jesus did not choose for Himself a visible abode on earth, but went up to Heaven and took His seat where we can see Him only with our spiritual eye, on the throne of universal dominion and majesty and might. Were He with us only in the body, we should frequently have to send for Him at a distance, when we desired His aid; and then He would often, as in the case of Lazarus, arrive too late to render us the wished-for help. In the event supposed, He could only show Himself in one locality at a time; whereas now

> "Where'er we seek Him He is found,
> And every place is holy ground."

His Spirit,—our Heavenly Guide and Monitor and Comforter,—is present in all places wherever called upon; and so we may approach Him when we please, and receive an answer to every earnest prayer.

This Jesus of Nazareth has acquired a fellow-feeling for us by means of the sufferings which He endured as a man upon earth; and hence, though now exalted to be a Heavenly Mediator between us and God, He is a High Priest who can sympathize with us in all our bewilderment, our trouble, and our grief. He feels for each of us that loves Him, and is trying to obey Him, the tenderest affection and concern; and we may be sure that, whenever we flee to Him, we shall obtain either the grace that delivers or the grace that comforts. Temptations, trials, sorrows, ought never to overcome us, or plunge us into despondency; for free and open is our access to Him who is easily "touched with the feeling of our infirmities" and pains. There is no ground here for hesitation and doubt. If we will only call to mind the tears which Jesus shed in the grave-yard of Bethany, His bitter lamentation over Jerusalem, His mercy displayed so wonderfully on Calvary, we shall certainly be persuaded that, glorified though He is, He still is moved with sympathetic tenderness and love. Clothed in our nature, and wearing that nature in the presence of the angels and of God the Father, He thinks just as much of us, and is as solicitous for our welfare, and regards us with the same sympathy, as He would, if He now sojourned among us in a visible bodily form. Is it not said of Him that He " ever liveth to make intercession for us"; and did not He Himself, after His resurrection and not long before His ascension, leave us these words of promise and consolation, "Lo, I am with you alway, even unto the end of the world." What more do we want to prove that, though in Heaven, Christ sympathizes with His friends upon earth, and means to perfect them, even if it be by suffering, for everlasting joy? Let us not despond, whatever comes; for Jesus is our sympathizing Comforter and Friend:

> " Our Fellow-sufferer yet retains
> A fellow-feeling of our pains;
> And still remembers, in the skies,
> His tears, and agonies, and cries.
>
> " In every pang that rends the heart,
> The Man of Sorrows has a part:
> He sympathizes in our grief,
> And to the sufferer sends relief."

It is just such a Saviour as the exalted Jesus that we guilty and disconsolate creatures need; and it rejoices us to know that He is pleading this day with His Father in our behalf. Oh, it is a soul-comforting thought that the Redeemer has even now the same compassion for our sinful race which He felt while dwelling upon earth. Sweet is it, too, to think that He has borne a human though glorified body within the vail of Heaven; and that there He sits, enrobed in a perfect humanity, upon the throne of unfading glory and undecaying power. This makes us sure that His sympathy with us is as warm, as tender, as close, as endearing, as ever; and tells us that His ear is always open to the call of our distress. Therefore do we approach Him with joy as our Heavenly Mediator,—as the One in whom the eye of our faith can behold the brightness of the Father's glory and the image of His person. In Him we discover all the severer attributes of the mighty and unchangeable God; and we find them sweetly tempered with infinite kindness and love. Our soul flows forth to Jesus thus exalted as a perfect manifestation of the Deity; and we bow before Him in holy reverence and awe. Oh, He has drawn very nigh to us by the assumption of our nature; and we feel that the words of comfort which He utters fall from lips that, having spoken formerly on earth, speak now from Heaven, and discourse most winningly of mercy in unison with truth and of righteousness harmonized with peace.

It may be that, when you think of the Father, you can not divest yourselves of the idea of God's terribleness; and that you are conscious of something about Him which is dreadful and dark. You can not help conceiving of Him as that awful Being who is invested with a might before which the heavens tremble and the earth rocks to its lowest seat; and as that awful Being whom the human mind can not comprehend in the midst of His mysterious and inaccessible grandeur. This view of God keeps Him away from you, as it were, and does not encourage you to open to Him the avenues of your heart. But, cease from such a mode of contemplation, and think of Him no more as an abstract and invisible Deity, but as a Deity embodied in the person of Jesus Christ, and made palpable to your senses in the form, the face, and the characteristics of a man. Think of the Deity thus; and your mind will be in perplexity about Him no more, your soul will shrink away from Him no longer with a feeling of dread, and your lips, expressing now the emotions of a heart delighted in His presence, will cry aloud with Thomas, "My Lord, and my God!"

In the person of Christ, transfigured and spiritualized as it now is, we can not but perceive the embodiment of the Father's attributes; and, as we think upon Him in this character, our souls are satisfied with His evident capacity to answer all our wants. Looking thus upon the Deity, we are conscious of no thrill of terror; but experience, on the contrary, an unspeakable sense of pleasure, and long to study more and more closely the mystery of that glorious nature in the contemplation of which our finite minds are utterly lost. We behold the same body which once tabernacled among men,—the same body which was ill-treated by its enemies, which fainted in the garden, which expired on the cross, which lay in the grave, which burst the bonds of death and ascended to the throne of the universe. It is the same body indeed; but it is that body etherialized, so to speak, and freed from every taint of mortal imperfection. Thus is it that the God whom we dare not look upon in His original brightness, unveils Himself to our spiritual sight. Divested in this way of the dreadfulness that hangs around Him, and clad in the robes of a divine humanity, He continually opens up to us a wider and deeper view into His character,—displaying new perfections, uncovering sources of mercy previously hidden, and spreading out before us a broader exhibition of His sympathizing love. Absolute Sovereign as He shows Himself to be, we are sure that He is the self-same Redeemer who lived a life of abasement for us on earth, who atoned for our sins by the spilling of His blood; and who, gifted now with all power, means to aid us in temptation, support us in trouble, and prepare us for the Paradise above.

Yes, this exalted Mediator, who is Deity incarnate, is a Saviour whom we all may love and may adore. He has the mighty power of a God and the warm sympathies of a man. Therefore He is as able as He is willing to save and to console to the uttermost all who come unto the Father by Him as a Mediator and Redeemer. Let us each approach Him, then, in faith, and give Him the homage, not only of our lips, but of our hearts and our lives. Then shall a stream of peacefulness and holy joy flow down from Him into our happy souls; and we shall bathe ourselves for ever in a flood of light and life and love.

A Sympathizing Saviour.

Christ Fitted by Experience to be a Sympathizer—Sympathy of Jesus ever Ready—Sympathy of Jesus All-powerful—A Blessed Record, "Jesus Wept"—Jesus a Sympathizer in our Poverty—Jesus a Sympathizer amid the Frowns of the World—Jesus a Sympathizer in our Temptations—Jesus a Sympathizer when we Feel Secret Anguish of Heart—Jesus a Sympathizer in our Mourning over the Wayward—Jesus a Sympathizer when Death Bereaves us of Relatives or Friends—Jesus a Sympathizer in all our Troubles—This Sympathetic Saviour Faithful amid our Unfaithfulness, and Faithful for ever—The Backslider and the Wavering Christian should Remember His Tears—The Impenitent should Weep in Regret, and Appeal to the Redeemer's Compassion.

A Sympathizing Saviour.

The heart of the Redeemer is full of sympathy for men in their fallen and exposed condition; for, when He lived in abasement on earth, He was compelled to undergo in His own person sufferings and trials and temptations of every kind. He knows the power and the keenness of them all; He knows their number, their fierceness, and their strength. He has counted them, has withstood the shock of their blast, has wrestled with the wrenchings of their might; and thus has He learned how to feel for those who are hard beset by trouble, and how to deliver them in their hour of pressing need.

And then in all this Jesus is just such a sympathizer as our heart longs to find, that it may pour forth before Him the story of its tribulations and woes. It brings us sweetest comfort to know that we have a Mediator in Heaven whose ear is ever open to our complaints, who hears them with willingness, and keeps the words we utter in constant recollection. Pleasing indeed is the thought that this same Saviour has gone through the furnace in which we are cast, has felt the beatings of the tempest which is raging round our head; and that, in consequence, the fluttering of our heart is but an answer to the fluttering of His heart, our pain the counterpart of His pain, our fear the image of His fear, our groans the echo of His groans, our tears the response to His tears. Faith and experience inform us that in Him we have a Friend to whom we may unbosom all our care, to whom we may recount the narrative of our troubles, and on whose sympathy we may always rely. Such a Friend is above the price of rubies and of pearls; and as compared with Him the finest gold of Ophir is nothing but dross.

The sympathy of Jesus with those who love Him is perfect. Not only was it to redeem them from the punishment due to their guilt that He put off the robe of His glory and came down to earth, but it was to fit Himself to be their Sanctifier, that so He might re-unite them the more closely to God. In His own person He went through all that we as Christians have to undergo, that He might become the more able to manifest sympathy to the sorrowing, and know the better how and when to send us relief. He sees our fears, He feels our anguish, He hears our plaintive sighs and our outbursting groans. And, if we come and lay our case before Him, He will administer suitable consolation, and speak the words of peacefulness to our agitated souls. We have only to approach Him with confidence, to fall in supplication before Him, and He will listen to the upbreathings of our prayer. Then will He call to us from Heaven in gentleness, and give us the assurance of His love. The calm voice of His sympathy will fall like a spell upon our softened souls. It will diffuse a holy charm around; and along the chords of our heart tones of heavenly music will thrill

> "Like the sweet melody which faintly lingers
> Upon the wind-harp's strings at close of day,
> When, gently touched by Evening's dewy fingers,
> It breathes a low and spirit-melting lay."

The sympathy of the Saviour is always equal to our need. Good is it at times to seek a human friend, and confide to him our troubles and our fears. He may, perchance, give us some solace, and say a word that will cheer our fainting heart. But we can find no such a comforter and adviser as Jesus among all our earthly companions. Troubled and anxious themselves, they are not always in a frame of mind which admits of their thinking of the troubles and anxieties of others. Their patience, too, though it may endure long, is likely to be wearied out with our constant coming; and their business may frequently prevent them from attending to our wants. It is not so, however, with the Friend we have above. He is always ready to listen to our complaints, seeing that He is the same in compassion yesterday, to-day, and for ever. His patience is exhaustless; and at no time is He so occupied that He can not attend to the petitions of all who draw nigh to the throne of His grace. Never was He known to neglect the supplication of the destitute or to despise their prayer. To every one that asks of Him He giveth liberally; for His heart is the store-house of pity, of gentleness, of condescension, and of love.

Besides this, the Mediator who feels for us so tenderly, has all power to comfort us and to bring us relief. Though the sympathy of Jesus should be strong enough and warm enough to melt our heart with responsive affection, yet could it never afford us perfect happiness, were we not assured that it is conjoined with ability to deliver us from all our woe. Kind as He might be, if He were also powerless as human friends so often are, He would not be, what He now is, all that our souls desire. His ear might be open to hear; but if His hand were shortened, so as to be unable to save, He would not be our refuge and our stay. He might weep when we wept; and yet, if His resources were not abundant enough to answer all our necessities, we would not apply to Him in every time of want, and ask Him to lighten the burden of our care. But, when we perceive, as we do, that to His wonderful sympathy is added infinite might; when we are assured that He will not only weep over, but heal, our wounds, that He will not only love, but soothe, our troubled soul; when we have learned that He has not the will alone, but also the power, to bring light out of darkness, and to chase away fear by the gladdening beams of hope; oh, when we perceive·all this, we feel that Jesus is every thing the heart can desire, and we cling to Him as the Friend who loveth at all times, and with more than a brother's love.

A cheering truth is this, fellow-believers in the Gospel, that we have in Heaven an all-powerful and ever-sympathizing Friend. Let us bless the record which tells us that " Jesus wept"; for here is a balm for every wound, a cordial for every care. There is not a sigh that stirs our bosom, there is not a pang that tears our heart, which finds not in His breast a quick response. His ear is always open to the story of our wretchedness; His eye is always ready to fill and overflow with tears. His heart is never weary with giving sympathy; His hand is never weary with imparting peace. All our trials, and our wants, and our wishes, and our hopes, and our feelings, have been His; and not a tremor have we had of anguish to which the chords of His spirit have not vibrated loudly and long.

Are any of us in poverty, and do we feel the pressure of want? Let us remember that our Lord was poor,—having no home of His own during His regular ministry, and having His necessities supplied by the kind liberality of friends. He was born in a place where beasts of travel were wont to lodge at night; He found shelter during His life of wanderings, sometimes beneath the roof of one who wished to hear His words of wisdom, sometimes not at all; and when He died, His body was embalmed with another man's spices, and buried in another man's tomb.—He is able to sympathize with us, therefore, if we have need of this world's goods, and feel the pinchings of destitution; and we may be sure that He is thinking of us in our distress, and will, in His own wise time and way, pour into our bosom the oil of comfort and of joy.

Are any of us frowned upon by the world? It becomes us, in such a case, to call to mind how our Master was reviled, and mocked, and rejected; how His teachings were slighted and contemned; how His example was disregarded, and even made the subject of false representation; how His admonitions were treated with rudeness and contempt; and how, at last, after multiplied insults and cruel torture, He was nailed in ignominy upon the cross. Therefore does He know how to feel for us, if we are exposed to ill treatment from those who hate us and would do us harm. Even the sting of ingratitude He is able to extract, and to soothe its fiery wound. He saw enough of this, and experienced enough of it, from those whom He sought to benefit by His instructions, and for whose spiritual salvation He sacrificed His dignity, His comfort, and His life. He remembers how His countrymen repaid Him for His heart-throbs of kindness; and He remembers, likewise, how even His favorite disciples forsook Him in the hour of His distress, and left Him to do battle with the powers of darkness all friendless and alone.

Are any of us encompassed by temptation? The Saviour has not forgotten the wilderness, and the conflict there waged by Him with Satan; nor has He forgotten the thousand arts and wiles of the Deceiver, and the malignity of His might. He has not forgotten Gethsemane, where Belial plied Him hard; nor the hill on which, while He hung quivering in agony from the cross, Belial shrouded His soul in clouds of darkness, and shut off from Him the sight of His God. We can know nothing of a temptation so terrible as that; and, if we could, Jesus would be able to sympathize with us in it, and to support us under the torturings of its attack.

Have we some secret bitterness of soul, some heart-anguish, which we can not impart to any earthly friend? While the Saviour sojourned in the flesh among His brethren, He had many an experience into which none who saw Him could enter, and which only His Heavenly Father could understand. He feels for us now just as His Father then felt for Him; and, knowing this corroding care that consumes us, He invites us to come and whisper it into His sympathizing ear. If we will only take Him at His word, and confide to Him our hidden distress, He will administer the desired comfort to our heart. He has erected a throne of sympathetic love in Heaven, and thither may we go with all the troubles which others can not comprehend; and, when kneeling there, we need keep no sorrow back, no trembling doubt, no anxious fear.

Do we mourn over the thoughtless waywardness of those who are dear to our souls, and whom, in spite of our warnings and entreaties, we see perishing in their guilt? It may be that when we have been most anxious for their welfare, and showed our anxiety the most, they have wounded us in our affections, and made us weep the tears of grief. Our Saviour knows how sad our bosom is; for He endured the same, and even worse, from some who called Him Friend. Nay, did not many of those who professed themselves His followers, and who seemed at one period to be as honest and as zealous as the others,—did not many of these become offended at what they called His "hard sayings," and kept company with Him no more? Were not even His own brothers vexed with His teachings; and did they not for a time withhold from Him the fullness of their confidence and faith? Ah, then, He is ready to sympathize with us in this form of our sorrow. Let us turn to Him, therefore, and ask for consolation, when our love is slighted, when our affectionate admonitions and beseechings are unheeded, and when they whom we long to benefit reject our proffered aid, and put aside the hand that would grasp their souls and rescue them from the burnings which are eternal. He will console us, and will assure our fainting hearts, saying to us for our comfort, "Sorrow not; ye have done your duty, and your garments are free from the stains of blood."

Has Death come into your family, and torn a loved one from your embrace? Consider Jesus weeping at the grave of Lazarus, and know that He is sympathizing with you in your bereavement. Tenderly does He gaze down upon you from Heaven; and, could He now weep in the midst of His glory, He would mingle His tears with yours. Look up into His face, and learn from His compassionate smile how ready He is to infuse the balm of comfort into your soul.

Art thou a father who hast been bereft of an infant child ere yet it had learned to lisp thy name and fling its tiny arms around thy neck? Or has the son who bore thy likeness been stricken down in ripening manhood, and left thee all childless and alone? Or has a daughter who brought to mind the image of her sainted mother been wrapped in her winding-sheet and laid away in the chambers of the dead? The Saviour pities thee, thou weeping mourner; and the throbbings of His heart answer back to the throbbings of thine.

Art thou a mother lamenting for the babe which fell asleep upon thy breast, and woke no more? Or is thy maternal bosom rent with anguish because of the innocent boy who will never again cheer thee with his merry laugh and playful ways? Or art thou grieving over the loss of the little girl who recalled the scenes of thy maidenhood, or the loss of the grown-up daughter who had just assumed the responsibilities and cares of married life? Be comforted, thou sorrowing soul. Thou art not forgotten by Him who has the power and the will to soothe the achings of thy woe. Seek Him, and ask relief. Then will He give thee "for mourning" "the oil of gladness"; and for "the spirit of heaviness" He will give thee "the garment of praise."

Art thou a husband sighing over the new-made grave of thy wife; and does it seem to thee that cheerfulness has fled for ever? There is one above who has compassion on thee, and will send thee comfort.—Art thou a widow left spouseless and friendless to struggle with adversity and to cower beneath the world's harsh frown? The Saviour knows the bitterness of thy heart; and, if thou wilt only make the request, He will turn the streams of that bitterness into the sweet outgushings of joy.—Art thou a child that hast followed the corpse of thy father to its long home, or buried the loved remains of thy mother "low in the ground"? Thou art bereaved indeed. But, forget not, in the tumult of thy grief, that Jesus is a father to the fatherless, and that He has more than the affection even of a mother for the children of His love.—Brother, hast thou been deprived of thine only sister; or, sister, hast thou been severed from thine only brother? Mourn not as though all were dead who think of thy welfare. There is an ever-living Friend in Heaven who feels for thee, and would ease the painful beatings of thine heart. Go to Him in supplication, tell Him of thine anguish; and He will give thee rest.

Come, thou that art bereaved, and look upon the Saviour who has a fellow-feeling with thee in thy woe. When thou didst lately consign the body of that cherished one to the tomb, thy heart seemed withered, a desolating blight came over thy soul, and thou didst feel forlorn and crushed to earth. Thou didst grieve greatly over thy loss,—perhaps too much ; and thou didst forget for the time, it may be, that there is a Friend in Heaven into whose bosom thou art entitled to pour all thy sorrow and complaints? Has He thus far escaped thy recollection? And hast thou forgotten even for a moment that He has the power and the will to speak words of comfort to thy soul? Uplift thine eye to Him now,—even to Jesus the Glorified and the Exalted ; and ask Him to send thee consolation and peace. Behold the mansion which He has prepared for thee in the midst of His own abode. Behold it; and wonder, and praise. Cease thy mourning, and tell thy tears to stop their flow. Yonder home of bliss was built for thee. Favored mortal, canst thou now find it in thy heart to murmur or repine ? Thou art journeying to the land where there is no more vexation, and no more anxiety, and no more sorrow. What to thee are the troubles of earth, when thou knowest that all of them will soon be swallowed up by heavenly joys ? Jesus, thy sympathizing Saviour, shows thee what His love will bestow upon thee ; and, while He points to thy promised inheritance, He bids thee cast all thy care upon Him, and wipe the drops of anguish from thine eyes.

Believer in Jesus, rejoice in the consciousness that, be thy trouble what it may, whether now or in the future, the exalted Mediator and great High Priest has a fellow-feeling for all thine infirmity and suffering and woe. When there are none on earth to whom thou canst repair for sympathy, thou mayst go to Him in the full assurance that the prayer of thy faith will be heard. Never yield to despondency, then, even though thy spirit be overburdened with its grief. Let distress and anguish come, if they will:

> " Still despair not : there is One
> To whom sad hearts have often gone.
> Though rich the gifts for which they pray,
> None ever come unblest away.
> Then, though all earthly ties be riven,
> Still smile : Thou hast a Friend in Heaven."

Yes, brethren beloved of the Lord, in whatever shape trouble attacks us, we may always draw consolation from the thought that we have an High Priest that is " touched with the feeling of our infirmities", and will never suffer us to mourn uncheered and alone. The reflection that Jesus wept on earth, and that His compassion is yet unchanged, will ever afford a solace to our bruised and wounded hearts.

Oh, what a Comforter this Saviour is! For more than eighteen centuries has He been soothing every variety of grief, and He has relieved trouble in every form which it has assumed. If the sympathy of a human friend can lighten, as we know it does, the load of our distress, how much more relief, and how much sweeter, may we obtain from the sympathy of Him who is God and has all the resources of the universe at His command? Think of the boundlessness of His compassion, and rejoice. Consider the fact of His coming from Heaven to earth to "heal the broken-hearted, and to comfort all that mourn." He loved His fellow-men; and He invited all of them who felt weary and heavy-laden to come to Him and accept of perfect rest. But chiefly did He show to His immediate friends the warmth and depth of His attachment. The disciples to whom He revealed the mysteries of His kingdom, could testify to us of the power of that affection which, having loved once, loveth to the end. Remember how He enlivened their faith when they began to doubt, how He dissipated their fears, how He endured their willfulness and their waywardness, and how He even forgave their desertion of Him in His hour of need. Though they often abused His kindness, He loved them still, and loved them always. He loved them while He was tried and tempted in the flesh; He loved them when quivering in the agonies of death; He loved them after He had risen from the tomb. The weeping Mary He comforted; to the desponding Apostles He came and spake the words of salutation, "Peace be unto you"; and, as He ascended in view of His disciples from Bethany into Heaven, He lifted up His hands and breathed upon them a parting but eternal benediction. He forgot them not when He took His seat upon the mediatorial throne, but sent down upon them in a copious and abiding outpouring the promised Holy Spirit, who should sanctify, and bless, and comfort them, and all His people, from age to age.

This exalted Jesus of Nazareth is just the Comforter whom we all need. There is a void within our hearts which He alone can fill; and there are pantings and longings of the soul which He alone can satisfy. None is there but Him to whom we can lift up our eyes as unto the hill whence cometh our help. He is our Mediator, and our only Mediator, for all time; and He is a Mediator who regards us in His exaltation with the same solicitude, the same sympathy, and the same affection which He manifested to His disciples when He tabernacled with them on earth. We know Him, and we acknowledge Him, and we rejoice in Him as the great High Priest who "ever liveth to make intercession for us" that love Him, and the sympathizing High Priest who is ever ready, when called on, to administer comfort to the sorrowing, to cure the sin-sick, and to make the wounded conscience whole.

Am I now addressing one who is a backsliding, or a wavering, Christian? If I am, let me entreat him to think upon the tears of the compassionate Saviour. O backslider! O waverer! what art thou doing? How is it that thou art turning again to the vanities of earth, when thou art aware that they are folly; and when, having known something of the powers of the world to come, thou hast learned that they are sweet to the spiritual taste and satisfying to the soul? Thou art forgetting thy Redeemer, and estranging thyself from His sympathy and love. A family altar lying in ruins, a closet of prayer unvisited, a Bible neglected, the ordinances of the Sanctuary attended with irregularity and attended with indifference, unite in proving that thou art trampling the blood of the covenant beneath thy feet, and art madly flinging the happiness of Eternity away. "Is this thy kindness to thy Friend?" Call to mind the weeping of Jesus in Bethany's graveyard; when, as He glanced down the long vista of coming ages, He saw the apostasy of every one who should desert Him, and rashly trifle with the once accepted riches of His grace. Think of the tears He then poured forth in the bitterness of His grief; and remember that among them all there may have been a tear for thee. Oh, that tear! that precious tear of the Saviour's! that tear forced up by anguish from His sympathizing heart! shall it have been shed for thee in vain? Backslider! falterer! stop in thy wayward and ruinous course,—stop, and reflect. Thinkest thou that Jesus has yet forgotten thee, or the tear He shed in thy behalf? Be assured, He has not. He is unchanged in His compassion for thee, though thou art sadly changed in thine affection for Him. He loves thee yet; and, if weeping were possible in Heaven, He would weep over thee to-day. Come back from thy guilty strayings, and seek His forgiveness for thine ungrateful neglect. Return, and cast thyself upon His breast. See how His eye is melting with pity at thy condition, and see how He beckons thee to come and fall into His open arms.

> "Return, oh, wanderer, now return;
> And wipe away the falling tear:
> 'Tis Christ who says, 'No longer mourn';
> 'Tis Mercy's voice invites thee near."

Perhaps I am addressing some hitherto obdurate soul that is now stirred with penitence at the thought of its long ingratitude towards the sympathizing Saviour? Is the one that reads these pages a sin-burdened spirit that has been aroused at length to a sense of its guilt and its danger, and feels itself exposed, and justly exposed, to the wrath of a righteous God? Mourner, whoever thou art, the sympathy of Jesus avails for thee. Believe this assurance, and act upon it, for it is true. Trust to His compassion, so abundant, so free; and seek for pardon through the Saviour without delay. Look for Him now; for, certain it is, thou hast, whether for time or for eternity, no other safe refuge, no other sure and solid hope.

Mourner, take courage from the record of the tears shed by the grave of Lazarus; and, going to Jesus at once, appeal to His compassion. Go, trembling with thy troubles; go, with thy guilt and shame oppressed ; go, even though thy sins look like scarlet, and rise mountain-high above thee ; go, tell Him all, and beg for pardon and for celestial life. Tell Him of thy deep soul-longings after forgiveness ; tell Him of thy doubts and forebodings ; tell Him how thy heart is desolate and wretched, and how thou art seeking some token of His sympathizing love. Fear nothing : He will hear thee. He heard the plaint of the blind Bartimeus, and He will surely listen to the story of thy woe. Plead His registered promise, "Him that cometh unto me, I will in no wise cast out": plead it fervently, and thou wilt prevail. Go to Jesus now, while He is calling thee : go to Him just as thou art, all sinful, all unworthy, and throw thyself in life-long consecration at His feet. Then will He smile upon thee tenderly, and, uplifting in His embrace, impart to thee eternal consolation and eternal rest.

Part Second.

The Tears on Mount Olivet.

"And when he was come near, he beheld the city, and wept over it, saying, 'If thou hadst known, even thou, at least in this thy day, the things which belong unto thy peace! but now they are hid from thine eyes.'"—LUKE xix. 41, 42.

———————— As He reached
The summit's breezy pitch, the Saviour raised
His calm blue eye: There stood Jerusalem!
. . . . There she stood;
Jerusalem,—the city of His love,
Chosen from all the earth; Jerusalem,—
That knew him not, and had rejected Him;
Jerusalem—for whom He came to die!—
The shouts redoubled from a thousand lips
At the fair sight; the children leaped, and sang
Louder hosannas; the clear air was filled
With odor from the trampled olive-leaves;—
But *Jesus wept.* . . . . . He only saw
Jerusalem, the chosen, the loved, the lost!
He only felt that for her sake His life
Was vainly given; and, in his pitying love,
The sufferings that would clothe the heavens in black
Were quite forgotten.—Was there ever love,
In earth or Heaven, equal unto this?

N. P. WILLIS.

Weeping over Jerusalem.

JERUSALEM FROM MOUNT OLIVET ON THE MORNING OF THE TRIUMPHAL PROCESSION—THE SAVIOUR'S PAUSE, AND HIS LAMENTATION OVER THE DOOMED CITY—PATHETIC GRANDEUR OF THE SCENE—JESUS WEPT OVER JERUSALEM ON ACCOUNT OF HER ABUSED PRIVILEGES AND HER CONSEQUENT PUNISHMENT—THE PEOPLE FOREDOOMED, YET MIGHT HAVE BEEN BLEST—PICTURE OF JERUSALEM'S HAPPINESS AND DIGNITY, HAD JESUS BEEN RECEIVED AS THE MESSIAH—THE OPPOSITE AND TRUE PICTURE—SOLEMN TENDERNESS OF THE SAVIOUR'S PLAINT—SORROW OF THE REDEEMER OVER JERUSALEM'S DOWNFALL AND THE NATION'S FATE—THEIR SPIRITUAL PERDITION THE CHIEF CAUSE OF HIS LAMENTATION—THE EXAMPLE OF JESUS TEACHES US TO WEEP OVER THOSE OF OUR NEIGHBORHOOD WHO OBEY NOT GOD AND CHRIST—OUR DUTY TO SAVE THEM BY OUR TEARS COUPLED WITH PERSONAL EFFORTS IN THEIR BEHALF.

Jesus Weeping over Jerusalem.

THE sun had risen upon Jerusalem, and was lighting up her house-tops, and her turrets and battlements, and the roof of her temple, with the blaze of his cheerful beams. Zion and Moriah and Acra were glistening in his brightness; and the mountains that girt "the holy city" were glowing beneath the splendor of his rays. The stars of the night had faded out; and the mists of the night had melted from around the hills and from the vales which lay below. The calm pool of Bethesda was beginning to shine as silver under the beams of the early sun; while the waters of Kedron sparkled like diamonds as they trickled down the ravine which divides Jerusalem from the Mount of Olives. The radiance of a lovely spring morning poured itself around the city of David,—a radiance whose brilliancy and warmth were tempered by a westerly wind that had come over the plain of Sharon from off the cool surface of the sea. The trees which stood upon the mountains, and along their sides, and at their base, and in the valleys, were waving with gladness in the breeze, and seemed to rejoice at the pleasantness of the opening day.

And now there began to be heard the hum of a city population awake from its sleep, and entering upon the varied activities of life. All Jerusalem was astir; for the hour of the morning sacrifice was past, and the duties of the day had begun. But while this busy scene was visible in the houses, and the streets, and the public places, of the city, a livelier drama was being enacted on the summit of the Mount of Olives. Jesus of Nazareth had arrived with a multitude of His disciples from the village of Bethany, and was about to make His triumphal entry into Jerusalem. He had reached the top of the eminence which overlooks the valley of Jehoshaphat and the hills beyond it. As he gazed around Him amid the splendor of that hallowed morn, He beheld not only the life-teeming city that sat below Him, but the blue mountains of Ephraim on the north and west, and the green hill country of Judea on the south, and the white summits of Moab in the east. Little, however, cared He just then for the grand natural prospect that was spread out before Him ; for that was not an hour which He could give to such a contemplation. He was proceeding to Jerusalem as her King,—going thither in the early part of that week whose close was to find Him crucified and in His grave. But the sounds which rose about Him were the sounds of triumph, and not of lamentation; and the acts that were performed before Him were the acts of homage, and not the last sad offices which prepared His body for the tomb. And now were heard loud shoutings of joy upon the top of Olivet, as the multitude strewed the path of the Saviour with their garments and with branches of palm ; and mighty was that burst of rapture which shook the hills around, when they cried out in the intensity of their adoration, "Hosanna to the Son of David ; blessed is He that cometh in the name of the Lord : hosanna in the highest!"

It is only for a moment that Jesus pauses upon the summit of the Mount of Olives. He soon begins to descend, heralded by the throng who would elevate Him to the throne of His father David. His eye is fixed upon the city ; and, as He thinks of her lost condition, there is sorrow in His heart. He has not gone far, when He checks the colt on which He rides, and gives vent to the feelings that trouble His soul. He sees no longer the animated faces of His disciples; He hears no longer the hymns of their praise; for His whole mind is absorbed in the fate of the people who have rejected His teachings, and are soon to deepen their guilt past hope of forgiveness by hanging Him on the cross. Often before has He approached Jerusalem by the same road, and looked upon it from the same spot; but never before have such emotions agitated His breast. He knows that it is the last week of her trial; and He foresees that she will certainly be condemned. His prophetic glance lights upon the gathering storm, and the doom both temporal and eternal which is to fall upon the city of His love. Therefore it is that, when He stops and gazes on Jerusalem, He weeps the tear of sorrow and divine compassion; and therefore it is that we hear from Him that mournful plaint which lays bare the agony of His heart, "If thou hadst known, even thou, at least in this thy day, the things which belong unto thy peace! but now they are hid from thine eyes."

There is another occasion on which the Saviour is represented as weeping; whereby it is proved to us that He was subject to the human feelings which move ourselves, and is therefore become a heavenly Mediator and High Priest just suited to our wants. That occasion was the death of His friend Lazarus, at whose grave Jesus wept in unison with the sorrowing Martha and Mary. There He shed tears of sympathy. Here we find Him shedding tears of disappointed affection and of mourning over those who desired none of His counsel and despised His reproof.

Some there are whose theology is cast in so rough a mould, that they are not pleased with this record of Jesus weeping over Jerusalem; and they see in it something not altogether harmonious with the inflexibility of the divine decrees. So wedded are they to their ideas about God's purposes that they are almost inclined to believe that Jesus ought not to have shed the tears of grief over sinners who were hopelessly undone. But this is carrying the metaphysics of Divinity too far. Rather would we range ourselves with those who look upon the narrative as one of the most pathetic of all that are related in the Scripture, and as not less true to the demands of a wholesome Theology than to the teachings of Nature. There is no scene more touching than this in all the New Testament, if we except the scene of Gethsemane and that of Golgotha. It is almost impossible to read the record, brief as it is, without being conscious of a powerful sympathy with the Saviour prompting us to pour out with Him the drops of grief. We feel that His was a love that was deep and strong; since, while it yielded to the demands of justice, it could not refrain from mourning over the fate of those who were to perish: and we rejoice to think that the same love fills His bosom now, exalted as He is to universal dominion, and gives assurance to those who are resolved to die in their sins that they are going down to the pit of the lost wrapped as it were in the fragrance of His lamentations. No other weeping teaches such a lesson as does the weeping of Christ over Jerusalem; for that must be agony indeed at which the Son of God is compelled to weep, when His own sufferings, now so nigh, could not wring from Him the tribute of a single tear.

It is not strange that Jesus wept when He gazed upon Jerusalem, and remembered her exalted privileges and her approaching doom. It was a city that had been highly favored of God upon which He looked down from the Mount of Olives. He called to mind the circumstances that had attended its foundation; and He recollected how it had grown to be the seat of the theocracy, and how its glory had been spoken of among all nations. As He cast His eye upon Zion, He thought of the palaces of its former kings. As He cast His eye on Moriah, He saw the magnificence of the temple, covered with plates of gold, ornamented with precious marbles, and looming forth under the rays of the sun like a "mountain of snow studded with jewels." In this temple, as He knew, dwelt the living God; and when that God should depart from it, the divine protection would no longer be vouchsafed unto Israel. Here had the daily sacrifice been offered up for a thousand years, and from this sacred sanctuary prayer had often ascended acceptably unto the Lord. The city had been the residence of many whom Jehovah had recognized as His servants; and it was the capital and the divinely appointed worshipping-place of the land which Jehovah had blessed, and had filled with the mementos of His presence and His protecting power.

Jesus remembered all this; but He remembered also how every one of these privileges had been abused. The miracles which Jehovah wrought of old had been forgotten; the Law delivered by Moses, and the instructions of holy men who spake as they were moved from above, had been either corrupted or disregarded; and even the teachings of the Messiah had been delivered to a hardhearted and gainsaying people. For more than three years had the holy Teacher who now wept over the city striven to lead its inhabitants to a knowledge of the truth, and to make them receive Him in His true character as a spiritual Saviour. He had instructed them out of the Law as one having authority ; but they were content with saying in wonder, " How knoweth this man letters, having never learned?" He had spoken to them of the free and full salvation which He was empowered to confer; but they only answered in their pride, "Have any of the rulers or of the Pharisees believed on Him?" He had warned them; but they had turned away in anger: He had entreated them; but they had only made their necks the stiffer in rebellion. All vainly had He toiled for them, and suffered for them, and prayed for them; and now just as vainly was He about to make Himself an offering for them, and for the redemption of a guilty world. He foresaw that as to them His sacrifice would be useless; nay, that it would only render their condemnation the more terrible and the more sure. The blood of the former prophets was calling out for vengeance against them; and to this there was soon to be added the cry of the blood that should stream from the cross. He perceived that the fate of the city was inevitable; and He could not but weep over the sad vision of its fearful downfall. He called to mind what Jerusalem might have been, had her people recognized Him as their King; and then in contrast with this, He looked forward, and saw what was soon to be her dreadful doom. No wonder that the sight unnerved Him; and no wonder that, in the anguish of His soul, He wept, and said, "If thou hadst known, even thou, at least in this thy day, the things which belong unto thy peace! but now they are hid from thine eyes."

It is true that Jesus knew from the beginning that the Jewish nation would reject Him, and bring down a merited ruin upon their own heads; and He was well aware that every step He took, and all that He said, was arranged upon the pre-supposition that they would refuse to acknowledge Him as the Messiah, and would even put Him to a shameful death. None the less, however, was He also assured that, had they accepted Him in His true character, and not blinded themselves to their destruction, then would their "peace have been as a river, and their righteousness as the waves of the sea." The structure of the sentence which He utters in His lamentation shows that He paused for a moment in the midst of it, and thought upon the happiness that would have fallen to the lot of His countrymen, had they only hearkened to Him and desired a knowledge of His ways. "If thou hadst known," He says, "even thou, at least in this thy day, the things which belong to thy peace",—" then," He means to intimate, "then it would have been well with thee, O Jerusalem; and thou shouldst have been the praise and the salvation of the world. Then, O Zion, city of the living God, thou shouldst have been glad in Me as thy Saviour and Redeemer; for I, even I, would have comforted all thy waste places, and have made thy wilderness like Eden, and thy desert like the garden of the Lord: yea, the glory of thy God should have risen upon thee, and Gentiles would have come to thy light, and kings to the brightness of thy rising."

It is pleasing to picture to ourselves, as Jesus pictured it to Himself, what might have been the result to Judea and to all the earth, had the Israelites as with one voice acknowledged Him to be the Messiah sent from God, and rendered Him the willing worship of their hearts. In such an event, the city of David would probably have stood in its beauty and strength to the present day, and all nations would now flow into it " to the house of the God of Jacob"; for then " out of Zion would go forth the Law" in a sense more literal than that of prophecy, "and the word of the Lord from Jerusalem."

Even under these circumstances, however, it would still have been necessary for Jesus to die; but His death would not have been brought about by the iniquity of His countrymen. He would have gone, perhaps, into the city and the temple during this last week of His ministry in the flesh, not to speak words of condemnation to a guilt-hardened race, but to tell to open ears and happy hearts the story of God's love, and to explain to all the mystery of redemption. He would have pointed out the necessity of His sacrifice as an atonement for the sins of His nation and of the world; and then, amid the tears of a sympathizing people, He would have publicly devoted Himself to death, perhaps upon the Mount of Olives in the full view of all, or perhaps upon the great altar of sacrifice in the court of the temple; where the sword of justice might have visibly gleamed forth from

Heaven and bathed itself in His blood. Then would He have been laid away in sad and solemn state in the tomb; but only to rise in majesty on the third day, and assume the personal dominion of Judea and of the world.

In such a case, the city of David would have become the excellency of many generations, the joy of the whole earth; and from her would have proceeded forth a righteousness which would long since have spread to the confines of the globe, and made all nations yield themselves in gladness to her mild and peaceful sway. Jerusalem would never have been trodden down by the Gentiles, and her land would not have been made the land of desolation. Had her people only hearkened to the voice of the Messiah, Judea would this day have been, it is likely, the first in every respect among the nations of the earth; and she would have been the country to which the whole world would be paying a joyful homage, as the cradle of Christianity, the seat of religion, and the chosen residence of Him who is " King of kings and Lord of lords."

This is a pleasing picture to look upon; but it becomes sombre and sad when we remember that it does not correspond to the truth. Jerusalem would not listen to the things which belonged to her peace; and therefore there came a destruction upon her proud palaces, and her gorgeous temple, yea, and her very foundations, that has made her name a by-word and a hissing for hundreds of years. Jesus had in view this withering desolation as He paused in His descent from the Mount of Olives; and the sight of it drew the tears of sorrow from His eyes. He would have turned it away, if He could; but He could not without doing violence to the claims of that justice which with Him were as strong as the yearnings of His love. He could mourn over a perversity which was bent upon self-destruction; but He could not pardon it after it had rejected the calls of Mercy till the day of Mercy was over. He looked, and saw Jerusalem surrounded by enemies that would burn her buildings, slaughter her people, and cast down her walls in the dust. There was no averting her doom; for her inhabitants, after being exhorted in vain to practise the righteousness that God required, were now, as He knew, about to fill up the cup of their guilt to the brim by crucifying the One who was sent to deliver them from their sins. He beheld before Him the imagery of a wrath such as had never descended on any nation; and His benevolent heart ached to its very core. As He looked upon the misery which was to roll down upon Judea, every feeling of tender recollection was stirred within Him; and He could not but utter that notable expression of sorrow which burst forth in tremulous tones of plaintiveness from His inmost soul.

These utterances of Jesus on the Mount of Olives are as touching as those which He spoke a few days later, on leaving the temple for the last time, when He exclaimed in words that were " musical in their sadness," " O Jerusalem, Jerusalem, how often would I have gathered thy children together, even as a hen gathereth her chickens under her wings,— and ye would not!" Just before this He had addressed the people in terms not only of sorrowful indignation but of stern rebuke,—menacing them with woe after woe, and telling them that upon that very generation should vengeance be taken for all the righteous blood which had been shed by them and by their fathers. It is at the close of these strong denunciations that He suddenly changes His tone from vehement oratory to the mild eloquence of plaintive grief, and concludes His harangue of awful thunder with that sweet lamentation over Jerusalem, which no one who has read it can ever forget.

Quite as tender, however, is the plaint which He utters when pausing in pensiveness amid His triumphal descent from Olivet, and weeping tears of distress over the fate of the city which He loved with all the ardor of His divine heart. There is something very solemn in that anguish which came upon Him in His hour of triumph, and made Him inattentive for the time to the acclamations which were sounded about Him by the multitude that cried, "Hosanna, hosanna; blessed is He that cometh in the name of the Lord!" And the solemnity of this anguish imparts a solemnity to the words which it forced from the Redeemer's lips, and sent down to us as an utterance of sorrow which, born itself of tears, is able to give birth to tears. There are few expressions so mournful in all the Bible. There is a melancholy in it that stirs the soul like the sad minstrelsy of woe. No funeral dirge is more plaintive; and no funeral music makes the heart-strings to vibrate more tenderly than do these words of touching grief,—"If thou hadst known, even thou, at least in this thy day, the things which belong unto thy peace!—but now they are hid from thine eyes."

You will not wonder at the sorrow herein displayed by Jesus, if you will but remember that

His prophetic eye was turned upon the scenes of Jerusalem's downfall and the wretchedness which was to follow. He saw Her wasted and desolate,—not one stone left upon another, and her inhabitants either weltering in their gore, or scattered over the face of the globe. The predictions spoken by Moses and by the prophets were, He perceived, very soon to be fulfilled; and there was to be accomplished also the yet more distinct prediction which He Himself intended soon to utter. That doleful cry, "His blood be upon us and upon our children!" sounded even now in His ears; and He was certain that such an imprecation must bring down before long a direful vengeance upon them who would send it up to Heaven in their mad impiety and guilt. Already He heard the tramp of the Roman legions, and the shriek of the Roman eagles hasting to their feast of flesh. He saw the beloved city beleaguered by a Gentile host, and her crowded inhabitants hemmed in on every side. He beheld Titus, the man of destiny, casting his first proud look upon Jerusalem from the hill Scopas, and then conducting the movements of the siege that ended in the city's overthrow. In His vision the Saviour looked upon Jerusalem as the prey of anarchy, of famine, and of the ravages of murderous war. He saw her houses filled with the dead and the dying, her streets flowing with blood, her towers overturned, her temple in flames, the fortifications of Acra and of Zion stormed, and all the city a scene of calamity, of carnage, and of death.

Yet farther did the Saviour look; and He beheld not only the overthrow under Titus, but the final overthrow in the reign of Adrian (135 A. D.), after which the Israelites were forbidden even to approach Jerusalem, and were kept out almost in a mass for two centuries from every part of the land of Judea. He gazed upon this last catastrophe in all its horrors; and He beheld at the same time the long series of abuses to which His countrymen would have to submit for the many weary centuries of their banishment from their ancestral home.

Such was the sight which passed across the vision of the Saviour, and made Him shed the tears of grief. Jerusalem rose up before Him as the spoiled, the desolate, the bound in chains. How could He do otherwise than weep, even as a patriot mourning over the desolation of His native land; and much more as a Redeemer who had come to seek and to save a nation that was spiritually lost and condemned to the sufferings of eternal woe? It was natural that He should grieve, as His imagination pictured forth the Roman driving his plowshare over the soil where once the temple had towered in its beauty and pride, and the Saracen building on its site a Mohammedan mosque; and it was meet that His soul should be stirred within Him, when He beheld Jerusalem's last conqueror, the stupid Turk, upturning her very ruins, violating the sacredness of her tombs, systematically insulting the descendants of those who in former days possessed Judea's realms, and treating with barbarian rudeness the followers of Him who is at once the prophet of Nazareth and the Redeemer of the world.

Jesus mourned over this; but much more did He mourn over the spiritual perdition which was to be poured upon Jerusalem and upon all the land. Observe the depth of His emotion, the keenness of His anguish; and you will perceive that the tears which the Saviour shed did not flow simply because the gorgeous temple on which He gazed from the slope of Olivet was soon to be burned with fire; or because the walls, and towers, and battlements, and palaces, of the city which shone before Him in splendor were soon to be leveled with the ground;

or because its inhabitants, then so full of life and so thoughtless of the future, were soon to struggle in the throes of physical death, or to be driven forth as a despised people among all the nations of the earth. There was a stronger reason than any of these for the Redeemer's grief, and a nobler source from which the tears of His compassion streamed. His lamentation sprung from the bitter consciousness that the woe that was coming upon the Israelites was a woe which would for ever affect the happiness of their souls. He foresaw the condemnation that would pass upon them in the day of the final judgment, of which the earthly judgment that was first to appear would be only a faint and feeble type. He knew that the sins of His countrymen would certainly plunge them into the gulf of perdition; and He could not but deplore aloud their bitter fate. The whole nation was posting on to ruin, for it had long been living in rebellion against its Maker and doing constant despite to the Spirit of His grace. The cup of its iniquity was almost full. One deed more,—the darkest deed of all,—and the Lord, provoked beyond endurance, would, as Christ was aware, discharge the vials of His resentment upon a people whom neither stern dealing, nor kind treatment, had been able to keep in their allegiance, or recall from the wanderings of their guilt. Oh, it was an awful retribution which was in sight; and, when He gazed upon it, Jesus, forgetting Himself as it were, gave way to a flood of compassionate tears, while the tender words of sorrow fell from His lips, "If thou hadst known, even thou, at least in this thy day, the things which belong unto thy peace!—but now they are hid from thine eyes."

Thus, Christian brethren, has the Saviour set us an example; and, if we will learn from Him, we shall be filled with anxiety for the salvation of those whom we know to be exposed to the punishment of eternal death. And it does seem to me that we should at all times, and chiefly now, be deeply concerned in particular for the fate of the neighborhood in which we reside. If we were assured that there is coming on a pestilence to desolate our homes, we should grieve at the announcement, and would be ready to weep in view of the suffering and anguish that are at hand. Why is it, then, that we are so indifferent to the spiritual fate of our friends and neighbors, when we know, as we do, that a disease is preying upon every one of them, which, if not checked, will for ever destroy their souls? Can we be Christians, and yet remain careless about this state of things, and forget the danger of the thousands who are living among us totally regardless of their eternal interests and of the claims of their God? I am sure that if the Saviour, again manifesting Himself in the flesh, should come and look upon that part of our land in which we dwell, He would weep over it as He wept over Jerusalem of old. He would weep to see so many that never hear Him spoken of except in blasphemy, and so many that care nothing for His claims, and so many that are daily hardening themselves against the calls of His grace; and He would weep to think that the whole of them,—the openly rebellious to His authority, and the neglecters of His salvation, and they who, knowing and feeling their duty, stand out in an increasingly stout resistance against Him,—yes, the whole of them, all that obey not His gospel, are hurrying on together in their blind infatuation to an eternity that is wretched and undone. Oh, brethren, if Jesus would weep over the ruined condition of these our acquaintances, and our friends, and our relatives, how is it that we do not shed for them the tears of grief; and how is it that we do not beseech them with all the earnestness of an agonizing heart to be forthwith reconciled to God? The Saviour is anxious in their behalf; and the angels are anxious in their behalf. And yet they are dying, eternally dying, because, perhaps, we are not sufficiently careful to warn them, and do not seek as perseveringly as we ought to pluck them as brands from the burnings of Gehenna. Some of these perishing sinners are our bosom friends,—our brothers, our sisters, our husbands, our wives, our children; and, as day after day passes by, and month after month, and year after year, they are, many of them, becoming only the more hardened to all admonition, and the more indifferent to the invitations of the Saviour's love, and the more neglectful of the kind offer of eternal life. Our entreaties with them and our prayers for them have been of no avail; and they are at this moment forcing their way through every barrier down to perdition, and heaping up to themselves wrath against the day of wrath.

Consider how pitiable is the condition of these neglecters of the Gospel. The Lord's anger is hot against them; and we can not tell how soon He may close the door of mercy, and leave them a prey to the adversary of their souls. Surely we ought to pour forth tears of anguish over them, and beseech them to flee from the ire of a sin-hating and sin-punishing God. Some of them are yet young, and are anticipating many years of pleasure; while at this very moment, perhaps, stern Death is putting his finger on the pulse of their life to still its beatings for ever. Some of them have reached middle age, and are yet so busied with the things around them that they give hardly a thought to the solemn Hereafter; while even now, it may be, the grave is opening to receive them in its cold embrace. Some of them have reached the very threshold of Eternity, and are still looking only at the scenes of earth; while it is certain that in a few more days they must hear their summons to the bar of judgment. Now, over the whole of these impenitent ones ruin impends, as we know; but, God forgive us! how feeble are our efforts, united or individual, to rescue them from their threatened doom! Alas! we seem almost indifferent to their fate; for scarcely a hand is stretched out in their relief, scarcely a heart is warm for their welfare, and scarcely a cheek is wet for them with the compassionate tear.

Think, brethren, think of the condition of these beings whom the Lord created for happiness, but who are madly consigning themselves to everlasting despair. You ought to pity them, to weep for them; for they are without God, and without Christ, and without hope. Oh, can you not shed over them the tears of grief,—such tears as Jesus poured forth from His compassionate heart? Heaven and earth might weep to see them walking in their blindness over liquid fires, and to see them insensible from their deafness to the sounds of condemnation that are muttering sullenly in the hot caverns below. If Heaven and earth might weep, surely you ought, each of you, to break forth in the words of Jeremiah's mournful plaint, "Oh that my head were waters, and mine eyes a fountain of tears, that I might weep day and night for the slain of the daughter of my people!" Lament, ye Christian men and women : lament, not for yourselves, but for those whom you see hasting on to destruction. Stop them with your tears; and implore them to think of God, of Eternity, of the world of bliss, of the dark realm of woe. Go forth weeping, every one of you : turn sinners from the error of their ways by your earnest supplications ; and they whom you convert shall shine as stars in the crown of your rejoicing for ever and for ever.

The Tears of Sorrow.

THE EXAMPLE OF JESUS A TEACHING INSTRUMENTALITY—HIS WEEPING OVER JERUSALEM AN EMINENT LESSON—THE REDEEMER'S SELF-FORGETFULNESS IN ALL HIS ACTS—THIS TRAIT BEAUTIFULLY SHOWN BY HIS LAMENTATION ON OLIVET—HIS OWN GRIEFS FORGOTTEN IN JERUSALEM'S COMING WOES—TEARS OF THE SAVIOUR INDICATIVE OF HIS INTENSE BENEVOLENCE—HIS LOVE EVEN TO HIS ENEMIES AND MURDERERS—LESSON OF KINDNESS AND GENTLE DEALING TAUGHT BY HIS EXAMPLE—THIS BENEVOLENCE NOT CONFINED, BUT WORLD-WIDE—OUR BENEVOLENCE SHOULD BE AS FREE AND AS LARGE—TEARS OF JESUS MANIFEST HIS DEEP SOLICITUDE FOR MAN'S SALVATION—IN THIS ANXIETY WE SHOULD SHARE—WHY CHRISTIANS WEEP OVER THE IMPENITENT.

Teachings of Christ's Sorrowing Tears.

THE teachings of Jesus of Nazareth are so much the more powerful because they are handed down to us, not only clothed in the words which He spoke, but exemplified in the whole tenor and conduct of His life. The religion He was sent to proclaim became incarnate in Himself; and He lived out in His own history every precept which He has enjoined upon them who wish to be made co-heirs with Him of the inheritance that is unfading and eternal. Hence it is that His example is put before us for our imitation; and we are encouraged to hope that, if we copy after it, and let the same mind be in us which was in Him, we shall be changed into His likeness, and be made partakers of His glory and His joy.

And it is most certainly our duty, as it ought to be our chief pleasure, to seek conformity to the image of the Saviour, by walking as He walked, and thinking as He thought. If we would learn what becomes us in any and every condition, it is only necessary that we look to Him who is the Apostle and High Priest of our profession, and by imitating whom we know that we shall approach nearer and nearer to that perfection unto which we are commanded to aspire. Thus may we learn from His example humility,—when we think of Him as "being found in fashion as a man," and cheerfully associating with the sinful, the degraded, and the lost; and we may learn obedience to our earthly superiors,—when we think of Him as "subject" to His parents up to His thirtieth year; and we may learn contentment with our allotment in the world, —when we think of Him as a homeless wanderer who often knew not where to lay His head; and we may learn active and unremitting benevolence, —when we think of Him as devoting the entire term of His ministry to deeds of kindness and love; and we may learn fervor of devotion,— when we think of Him as spending whole nights in prayer; and we may learn submission to the will of God under every dispensation of His providence,—when we think of Him as bowing meekly to the purposes of His Father in Gethsemane's garden, and drinking on Golgotha, and drinking without complaint, the wine cup of His Father's retributive wrath.

There is no incident recorded in the Saviour's history that does not teach us lessons of value; and this is peculiarly true of the narrative which tells us of His weeping over the city that had refused to receive Him as her Prophet, her Priest, and her King. Some of the most striking traits of His character are here brought out prominently into notice, and made to shine forth in a light as clear and soft as that of the sun's first morning rays. As we gaze upon this picture of sadness, and hear the plaint of Christ, we are struck by the whole scene as a wonderful exhibition of self-forgetfulness, of intense and all-embracing benevolence, of a deep solicitude for man's salvation, and of an earnest sincerity that would save sinners, if possible, from the wretchedness of everlasting destruction.

If we except Jesus of Nazareth, the world has never known a man perfectly free from the taint of selfishness,—one who has not sought his own happiness more eagerly and constantly than he has sought the happiness of others. In this respect the Saviour stands alone. Trace the course of His life from its beginning to its end; and you will find everywhere in it the most convincing proof that He cared not to advance Himself, but was wholly absorbed in promoting the welfare of those whom He came to seek and to save. His fixed and changeless aim was the working out of man's redemption; and never did He lose sight of it, though it led Him into ignominy, into suffering, and finally unto death. You know that He was offered worldly wealth, but refused it, that He might give spiritual riches to the spiritually poor; and you know that He was offered worldly dominion, but refused it, that He might establish a heavenly reign under which the heavenly-minded should be made kings and priests unto God. There was placed before Him the glittering bait of ambition; but the eye that beheld man's misery, and pitied it, could not be dazzled with the gleam of a bauble. There were spoken to Him the words of flattery; but the ear that was open to the cry of distressed humanity, was deaf to so paltry an enticement. These things turned not Jesus for a moment out of the path which He had resolved to tread; for it was not for Himself that He was living, and it was not for Himself that He purposed to die.

The trait of self-forgetfulness now spoken of, while it is seen in all the Saviour's doings and sayings, manifests itself at times in a manner that fills us with wonder, and makes us say aloud in the intensity of our emotions, "Truly, this was the Son of God!" When we observe Him, wholly unconscious as it were of His native dignity, reclining at meat with hated publicans and notorious sinners, and addressing words of tenderness to those who have cast off all goodness from their lives and dislike it in their hearts; when we perceive Him, even at a time in which men are seeking to show Him unwonted attention, turning away from them to put His hands upon the youth who desire His blessing; when we behold Him on the occasion of His last Passover comforting His disciples, while His own sufferings are totally forgotten; when we hear Him, as He staggers beneath the weight of His cross, saying to the women who lament His cruel fate, "Weep not for Me, but weep for yourselves and your children"; when, finally, we see Him even in His death agony anxiously mindful of the matron who gave Him birth, and commending her to the friend that had lain on His bosom; when, I say, our attention is called to these amazing instances of the Saviour's self-forgetfulness, we are thrilled with admiration, and can not but wish that we too might thus rise superior to our imaginary personal interests, and lose ourselves as completely as did He in the work to which we are divinely appointed.

Feelings like these rise up within us in a welling tide, when, in particular, we contemplate the self-forgetfulness exhibited by our Lord as He checked His progress down the Mount of Olives, and, casting over Jerusalem a look of sadness, let fall for her the tears of grief. There He stood in the hour of His triumph, while the expressions of homage were poured out before Him, and the acts of homage were busily performed; there He stood, and bowed His head, and wept. These which He shed were not the tears of mortified pride, called forth by His knowledge of the final rejection He would meet with from His countrymen; and they were not the tears of complaint toward God, because God had imposed upon Him a burden too painful to bear. They were the tears of anxiety, of disappointed love, and of sympathizing grief.

It was a mournful sight to behold Jesus stop amid the universal joy, and gaze upon the city, and shed over it the tears of a sorrowful heart. As He looked down from Olivet, He saw the garden in which He was soon to sweat as it were great drops of blood; and He saw the house of the high priest, where He was soon to be buffeted and mocked; and He saw the palace of Herod, in which He was soon to be treated with indignity and scorn; and He saw the prætorium of Pilate, where He was soon to be unrighteously condemned and ignominiously scourged; and He saw horrid Calvary, that gloomy " place of a skull", on which His body was soon to be racked with torture and the life-stream to gush in a torrent from His heart. He saw all these objects; but He saw as though He did not see. It was not the sight of them, sad as it was, that drew the tears of sorrow from Jesus' eyes. It was the prospect of Jerusalem's speedy downfall, and the thought of her people's everlasting ruin, that wrung from Him the drops of woe. The grand and venerable temple that loomed up before Him with its snow-white front and glittering roof, the massive city walls with their battlements and turrets, and the whole of Jerusalem with her terraced gardens and her mansions of magnificence, were in a few short years to be totally overthrown and piled one upon another in heaps of desolation. He mourned over the coming destruction as a native-born Hebrew, to whom Jerusalem seemed as " the joy of the whole earth"; He mourned over it as a man of compassion, who could not look on misery without a sigh;

and He mourned over it as a divine Saviour, who would have rescued His people from endless ruin, had they been willing to accept His terms of salvation. He could not think of the approach of the threatened desolation, and remain unmoved; and therefore it was that He stopped in the midst of His triumphal entry into Jerusalem, and, forgetting the woes that were preparing for Himself, cried out in the bitterness of His anguish over a city that might have been saved, but would not, "If thou hadst known, even thou, at least in this thy day, the things which belong unto thy peace!—but now they are hid from thine eyes."

There is another lesson taught us by the sight of Jesus weeping over Jerusalem; and it is a lesson of intense and all-embracing benevolence. It does not surprise us when we are informed that Christ wept at the grave of Lazarus; for Lazarus was His friend. Nor would it surprise us, had we been told (as we are not) that He shed tears over the bier of the disconsolate widow's son, or over the body of Jairus' maiden daughter; but it does surprise us to find it written that He wept at the fate of those who had repeatedly rejected His teachings, were about to do it again, and were moreover plotting even then to bring Him to a death of shame. But, if we are surprised, we are also gratified; for thus are we led to look upon Jesus putting His own precept into practice, and showing us by His example how we may love our enemies, and bless them that revile us, and do good to them that hurl at us the darts of envy and persecution.

In this remarkable conduct of the Saviour's we see displayed an intensity of benevolence to which all history can furnish no parallel. There is manifested a goodness of heart, a comprehensiveness of love, a depth and tenderness of sympathy, which can only be the affection of that God who gives His sun and His rain alike to the unjust and the just. This is philanthropy indeed, that can weep over the worst of foes, and grieve at a fate which their wickedness has well deserved. Already had the Saviour sacrificed much in behalf of His countrymen,—relinquishing every personal comfort to promote their highest happiness, and going about among them to do them good in the healing of their physical ailments, and in ministering to the wants of their souls. He had done this, not with that stern inflexibility of manner and that vehemence of speech which have always marked worldly-minded reformers, but in the calm gentleness of friendship, and in the mildness of love. Notwithstanding all, however, the nation had refused to receive Him as the Messiah of God, had put Him away with ingratitude and contempt, and was very soon to insult Him more cruelly than ever, and to rob Him of His life.

Jesus perceived the whole of their baseness; and yet in full view of it He wept over the doom of those who had rejected Him, had trampled His kindness under foot, and despised His well-meant admonitions and reproofs. The ingratitude of His fellow-Hebrews must have stung Him to the quick; but it did not seal up the fountains of His pity and love. Nay, even the intenser wickedness they were about to perpetrate against Him, and all of which He distinctly foresaw, availed not to quench His compassion; and the tears which He now poured forth over their guilt and its punishment were only an outgushing of that same sympathy which caused Him to pray for His murderers as they were nailing Him to the cross, and made Him instruct His disciples, after His resurrection, to begin at Jerusalem when they entered upon the work of preaching repentance and remission of sins unto all the world. Though His countrymen had abused Him, and reviled Him, and misrepresented Him, and cast out His name as evil, He loved them still; and, when He looked upon them and reflected on their lost condition, He felt as though He could bathe them in the tears of His outbursting grief.

Jesus of Nazareth, the sinless, wept over the guilt of those who had wandered from the paths of right, and He gave way to lamentation in view of the woe that was to effect their destruction. He wept over them, though they had done Him most cruel wrong; and He wept over them, though He was certain that their fate was fixed, and tears could be of no avail. How much more ought we, who are sinners ourselves, to weep over the errors of our fellow-sinners, when, as we know, the most of them have done us no harm, and when, as we have reason to believe, our tears, if seconded by our efforts, may bring them to repentance and to a reconciliation with God. We ought to grieve for our brethren who have slipped down into the pitfalls of sin, and, instead of reviling, we ought to extend to them the helping hand. Some of them, perhaps, are even now lamenting their folly; and, if we would only show them sympathy, they would strive to recover themselves out of their present pitiful condition. There are many that err, many that sin; and not a few of them are so hardened in their iniquity that it may seem useless to strive to reclaim them, and lead them in faith to Christ. But how know you that they may not still be redeemed? Seek them, and try upon them the power of tears. Deal gently with them; for they are weak, and frail, and sensitive to harshness and threats. Woo them with the tender words of love. Show them in kindness where it is they stand; place death before their eyes, and judgment, and eternity; and then implore them even with tears, if tears *will* flow, to flee from the wrath to come, and to lay hold on eternal life. Weep for them, when you pray in private in their behalf; weep, if Nature tells you, when you plead with them in person, and be not ashamed of exhibiting that kind of weakness which has often proved the magic of power when all besides has failed.

This weeping of the Saviour over Jerusalem,—over those who had most bitterly opposed the setting up of His spiritual kingdom,—is indicative of that wider benevolence which He has displayed to all the nations of the earth. It is true that Christ's personal ministry was confined to the Jews, and that His own labors, with hardly an exception, did not extend beyond the confines of "the lost sheep of the house of Israel." It is no less true, however, that the end of all He did was to have salvation preached in His name to every people upon the face of the globe. This was the object of His life and the object of His death. He came to redeem the whole world, and not Judea alone, from the enthrallment of sin; and all His ministry was so ordered that after His resurrection the Gospel of salvation should be proclaimed in every language and throughout every land. Compassion for humanity at large was the master force in His soul. And we can see it even here in His lamentation over the city that was doomed so soon to fall. From this we perceive that He loved men as men; and by how much He loved them, by so much He grieved to behold them hurrying on to an Eternity of darkness and despair. Think you that it was simply because the Jews were members of the same race as Himself, and of the same country, and of the same religious creed, that He wept over their approaching ruin, and mourned for their folly in not attending at the proper time to the things which belonged to their peace? Oh, no: He wept over them as men who were partakers of like flesh and blood with Himself,—as men who, though fallen and ruined, might have been upraised from their sinfulness, and made the heirs of never-ending life,—and yet as men who had madly put away from them every offer of celestial bliss.

Thus are we shown the wide reach of Christ's benevolence ; and we are called on in this particular to imitate His gracious example. Here we learn what was the estimation in which He held the human soul ; and we learn how deep and all-pervading was the interest which He felt in the character and condition of man, wherever found. It is evident that He saw in humanity, degraded and wretched as it is, powers that are still wonderful even in their ruins ; and it is clear that He longed to see men elevated to a communion with Himself, and grieved to behold them the prey of an ignorance and sinfulness which must at last consign them to the burnings of eternal shame. Yes, He pitied man in His lost estate, He had compassion on the multitude that were " scattered abroad as sheep having no shepherd"; and the thought of their spiritual condition and their awful destiny lay heavy on His soul. Jesus knew but too well that condemnation had come upon our race ; and, when He foresaw how many would fall in future years after the example of His own countrymen, and how many would, like them, refuse to wash in the fountain that has been opened for sin and for uncleanness, there beat the throbs of anguish in His heart, and tears gushed down His cheeks.

The spirit here manifested by Christ ought to move us each to sympathy with those who in our own or in other lands are walking in their impenitence to the grave. How few of us who enjoy the blessings of the Gospel feel in this matter as the Saviour felt when He was weeping over Jerusalem, and as He feels even now when seated in majesty on His throne. Look around you, and tell me where among professing Christians is that anxious love for the erring and the lost which Jesus manifested when He poured out His sighs and tears upon the Mount of Olives. Oh, were we filled with this love, and were we moved by its mighty impulses, we should not suffer so many of our friends to remain unwarned in their iniquity, and be content to shed those tears over their tombs which had better been shed over their lives ; and we should not let the heathen of foreign countries be sitting unprayed for in their dark alienation from God ; and we should not be ever attentive to the news that comes from far-away lands respecting the ravages of pestilence and war, but always indifferent to the oft-repeated story of their spiritual destitution and guilt; and we should not be so eager to provide for ourselves a superabundance of the meat that perisheth, when we know that millions both at home and abroad are famishing for want of "the bread of life."

If these things fail to touch us, it is because we do not sympathize with Christ, nor with those for whom He wept. Jesus felt, and felt deeply, for man's ignorance, and weakness, and guilt. He grieved over the whole race, and sighed to think of their awful doom. And yet there was one respect in which He could not sympathize with humanity as can we. "He knew no sin"; but we know it, and, oh! we know how bitter it is, and how vile, and how degrading, and how entirely it shuts us out from communion with God. Now what our condition was before we were washed and sanctified, that is the condition of all the unconverted; and in that they will for ever remain, if they do not come to Christ and receive from Him the gift of pardon and eternal life. Can we know this, and yet not be anxious for them; can we know it, and yet not weep over them such tears of sorrow and compassion as Jesus wept? God forgive us, if we have hitherto proved recreant in this matter to our trust; and may we now, if never before, go forth in tears to the work of warning sinners, and of saving them, if possible, from the groanings and writhings of undying remorse.

Whenever we call to mind this picture of Christ weeping over Jerusalem, we can not but be impressed with the conviction that He was wrought upon by a deep solicitude for man's salvation. There is no avoiding the belief that the conversion of all men is the object that lies closest His heart; and that we, therefore, who are His disciples should look upon the regeneration of the world as He looked upon it from Olivet, and afterwards from Calvary, and now from the battlements of Heaven. Jesus heard the roar of a coming desolation; He saw its shadow creeping on; and He wept over those who were devoted to destruction the tears of compassionate grief. And this ought we to do, when we see the ruin that is hanging over them that are dear to us, and threatening every instant to make their repentance vain.

Brethren, it is not strange that we should feel anxious in view of the danger to which our unconverted friends and all the impenitent are exposed. It would be strange indeed, if we did not; and it would be very pitiable, if we never felt the tear of anguish welling up at the thought of their probably miserable doom. By their own confession these unpardoned ones are not happy now, and there is but little prospect,—none whatever, if they do not flee to Christ in faith,—that they will be happy hereafter; for all that they are doing, and wishing, and planning, and resolving, is only calculated to consign them the more surely to the dungeon of despair. How can we behold them thus careless, and not give way at times to a flood of tears? Oh, it is impossible to observe their growing indifference to the invitations of the Saviour, and their increasing callousness of soul, and their ever-strengthening mad determination to perish in their guilt, without groaning in spirit, and being impelled almost to say of each of them, as said Jesus of sin-ruined Jerusalem, "If thou hadst known, even thou, at least in this thy day, the things which belong unto thy peace!—but now they are hid from thine eyes."

Think it not an uncalled-for thing, O ye impenitent, if ministers and Christian friends weep over you, and urge you with tears to attend to the matters which pertain to your salvation. Did you see what we see, and know what we know, and feel what we feel, your only wonder would be that we do not show even greater anxiety about your spiritual welfare, and do not beseech you with a more urgent pertinacity to turn from your unrighteousness, and live. Oh that we who are the followers of Jesus might be more faithful to you than we have ever been, and might tell you with more of earnestness, and more of tenderness, and more of weeping compassion, that, if you change not your course, you are utterly ruined and lost!

I am afraid that some of you to whom I now speak are turning yourselves into "vessels of wrath fitted for destruction"; and all because you will not be persuaded to repent of your iniquity, and believe in Christ. It is my heart's desire and prayer to God for you that you may be saved; but I am awfully anxious lest, notwithstanding all that has been done for you and upon you, you may become by your continued disobedience the heirs of eternal misery and disgrace. Oh that I could now speak to you with the overwhelming might of an Edwards, or rather with the winning gentleness of a Payson or a McCheyne, and be made the instrument of converting you to Christ! I think that I sincerely believe the Gospel; but I know that in me, as in no man, is there power to create the faith of it in your hitherto cold hearts. And yet the Gospel is eminently worthy of your belief and of your love. Now, how can you be made to believe it and obey it? If it would avail any thing, I could tell you with tears of the dreadful curse which is resting upon your souls, and of the unquenchable fire that is burning for you in the lowest depths of the nethermost world. I could tell you also, and tell you weeping, of the coming judgment, and ask you all, " What will ye do in the end thereof?" And more than this could I tell you. I could portray to you the infinite compassion of the Saviour, and could picture forth before you that mercy of His which has never failed. Let me remind you of these things now in this the day of your visitation and acceptance. Will you not listen to the beseeching entreaties of the Redeemer; and, as you have never yet cared for His threatenings, will you not now be melted by His tears? Give heed at once, I beg of you, to the things which belong to your peace; for, if you persist in neglecting them, the time is certainly at hand when they will be hid from your eyes.

Lamenting Over Sinners.

The Weeping of Jesus on Olivet a Proof of the Sincerity of His Wish to Save the Guilty from Ruin—The People over whom He Wept He had Labored for in Love; and hence His Tears—Consistency of this Grief with the Fact (well known to Jesus) that the Jewish Nation was Devoted to Destruction—Repentance would have Saved the People; but, not Repenting, they were Lost by their own Fault—Invalidity of the Sinner's Excuse that his Fate is Pre-determined by God—The Impenitent Man Self-destroyed—God's Offer of Salvation to All a Sincere Offer—Every Man Invited in Various Ways to Look in Penitence and Faith to Christ for Salvation—Tears of Jesus Still Appealing to the Sinner—The Weeping of the Redeemer Manifests the Dreadfulness of the Doom of those who Reject His Love—These Tears Forebode the Sinner's Eternal Destruction—Now is the Time to Seek the Saviour; Now, while God has not Hidden the Things that Pertain to Man's Peace.

The Saviour's Lamentation over Sinners.

It has been shown that the weeping of Jesus of Nazareth over Jerusalem, after its inhabitants had openly and often slighted His teachings, and when they were soon, as He knew, to deliver Him up to crucifixion, is a striking manifestation of His self-forgetfulness, and of His benevolence, and of His solicitude for man's salvation. His tears prove yet more; for they evince, as has been intimated, an earnest sincerity on His part that would rescue the guilty, if possible, from eternal ruin. Had they been merely human tears, this might be doubted; but, being the tears of the Son of God, who can not deceive, they may well be taken as a true indication of the feelings of His heart. Jesus would never have wept, had He not seen something, or felt something, which called for tears. The moving that stirred Him to His soul was a moving of sincerity; and it told even more plainly and emphatically than words could tell how unwilling He is that sinners should perish, and how grieved He is whenever, in despite of His wishes and His express invitations, they are determined to die.

For more than three years had the Saviour exercised His ministry among the people of His nation,—healing them that were afflicted with diseases, restoring the blind, the deaf and the lame, calling the dead to life, working marvellous miracles, and preaching the Gospel of the kingdom of God and Christ. All of these things had He done in Jerusalem, or in its neighborhood; and there were many in the city who were acquainted with Him as a man of mighty deeds, and some that believed Him to be the Messiah who was to come into the world and reign over every nation on the globe. He knew the people well; and He loved them with all His heart. They were endeared to Him, partly because they were, like Himself, the descendants of Abraham, partly because they were the chosen of Jehovah, and partly because He had labored and suffered in their behalf; but they were dear to Him chiefly because they were straying off from Him who was the Heavenly Shepherd and Bishop of their souls.

It is not strange, therefore, that, as Jesus stopped for a moment on the slope of Olivet and surveyed the city into which He was about to enter for an hour of brief triumph, He could not refrain from weeping over the recollection of her folly in disregarding His claims, and over the vision of her approaching destruction, and the eternal fate of her guilty and blood-stained inhabitants. He looked down upon a people who deemed themselves wise, when they were rejecting wisdom's Author; who were constantly neglectful of their dearest interests; and who, while living under a blaze of light, were so self-blinded by infatuation that they could not recognize Him whom God had appointed to be their Deliverer, and through whom God was ready to make them more fully than ever the nation of His choice regards. He perceived that His teachings had been in vain, and in vain His doings of miraculous might. The tempest was brewing; the clouds of divine wrath were collecting; the thunders were muttering in the distance; and very soon, as He foresaw, the gathering storm of indignation would burst, and pour down ruin on all the land. It was to Him a grievous sight, and when He gazed upon it, He heaved a sigh, and wept.

You may be sure, then, that these which Jesus

shed were not the hollow tears of show, but tears of sincerity that came welling up from an aching and disconsolate heart. They spoke volumes of tenderness to those who saw them as they flowed; and even yet, speaking to us, as they do, of a love that clings to us in our guilt, and weeps at our woe, they have not lost the witchery of their original fascination over the feelings of the soul.

It may strike you, at the first thought, as somewhat singular, that the Saviour should mourn, and mourn sincerely, as if it were a thing that might have been avoided, over a destruction which He knew to be determined upon in God's counsels, and without the occurrence of which God would seem to have been thwarted in His plans. Though He was well aware what agency His countrymen would take in His death, and was also aware that for this and their other guilt they should be uprooted from Judea; and though He understood perfectly that they would never repent of their transgressions against a merciful Sovereign, and would never believe in Him as the promised Messiah, Jesus kept plying them to the end of His ministry with entreaties, and warnings, and expostulations, just as He would have done, had it still been wholly doubtful to Him whether they might not yet look with loathing upon their iniquity and acknowledge Him as their King. He did this because He knew that, notwithstanding God's purpose of working by their agency, the Israelites were entirely at liberty to choose their own course, and at liberty to act as they pleased. There was no constraint put upon them at all; for what they did was done at the dictate of their own will; and, so far as it was wrong, they alone were responsible for the guilt.

What precise object the Saviour had in keeping on with his pleas when He perceived they were vain, we may not know,—unless indeed it was to prove to all subsequent ages that the Jewish nation lost His favor solely by their own fault, and after He had urged them by every consideration to pause in their mad career, and to turn from their wicked course. We do know, however, that He was altogether sincere in His offers; and that, had the Jews hearkened to His call, the nation would not have been blotted out from the land, and the people would not have perished eternally in their sins. If they did not obey Him, it was by no means because they *could* not, but simply and solely because they *would* not. They might have given heed to His admonitions and His invitations; but they wished it otherwise; and otherwise it was. While, therefore, it is true, on the one hand, that the rejection of Christ by His countrymen had entered into the calculations made by God before the world was created, and true that the redemption of the human race depended in some sense upon their crucifying the Lord of glory; it is not true, on the other hand, that this arrangement of God's made their wrong-doing necessary,—since they would have done what they did, whether God meant to employ their agency in the furtherance of His plans or not. Their whole acting was of their own free will, and only at the promptings of their own evil hearts. Hence they were without excuse for putting the Saviour away from them; and the Lord was just in His stern reckoning with the whole nation for spilling the blood of His Son.

Just so is it with all God's dealings with men. He makes use of them,—of their wicked no less than of their right actions,—to bring about the accomplishment of His own designs; but He always does this in such a way that their freedom is not interfered with, and their guilt, if they sin, is all their own. It is idle then for you who are impenitent to plead, as sometimes you do, that you can not be different from what you are, and that, if you are finally lost, it will be, not because of any fault in yourselves, but because God had ordered it so, and determined upon your death. It is undeniable that He who made you knows perfectly, and always knew, what will be your eternal destiny; and He could not be more certainly informed of it, were it even fixed irrespective of your conduct by an absolute decree. But you will recollect that God's foreknowledge puts no restraint whatever upon your actions,—that you are consciously free to do as you please, and just as free as you would be if God had no connection with you at all. If you hearken not to the things which pertain to your peace, it is because you *will* not hearken; and if, in the face of all your well-understood obligations, and in the midst of your Gospel privileges, and in despite of the repeated admonitions of God and the multiplied entreaties of Christ and the frequent soul-drawings of the Spirit, you continue to oppose yourselves to the invitations of divine love until you are given over to blindness of mind and hardness of heart, it will all be because you *would* not listen to the beseechings of a weeping Redeemer, and *would* not accept of His gracious salvation.

You have the power to obey the Saviour's call. You feel that you have the power; and you feel it none the less, even though God may be certain on His part that you will never exert it, but will go down in your impenitence to the pit of perdition. It is not power, then, that you lack : it is *will*. Your will is perverse; moved neither by the kind words which Jesus speaks to you, nor by the tears which He sheds over your obstinacy and wicked unbelief. Be not deceived. Yourselves alone are to blame for your holding out against the invitations of the Saviour's love ; and oh ! let me tell you, the hour is hasting on, and may be even now at hand, in which, if you persist in your rebellion, the overtures of mercy will be made to you no more, and when He whom you have so wrongfully slighted will offer no longer to gather you beneath the shelter of His wings, but will say to you in the words of a sorrowful parting, "If ye had known, even ye, at least in this your day, the things which belong unto your peace !—but now they are hid from your eyes."

Doubt as you may, there is nothing more certain than that the Saviour is sincere when He offers you salvation. He does not want any one of you to perish ; and, if you will perish in spite of His wishes and His entreaties, you will go down to the dark dungeon mourned over by His sympathetic heart, and lamented for as the miserably and eternally lost. You ought to know this, and to feel this; for such is the lesson taught you by the weeping of Jesus over the doomed city of His love. And that same Divine Friend who wept at the fate of Jerusalem, is even now looking down from Heaven upon each of you, and He says, "Oh that thou wouldst know, at least in this thy day, the things which belong to thy peace!" If you will not obey His call, it is because you do not believe in His sincerity, and are distrustful of the offer of His grace. Credit my assertion when I assure you that Jesus is in earnest,—that He wants to draw you to Himself, that He wants to reconcile you to God, that He wants to whisper words of hope and peace to your souls. There is no one of you who is not called, and no one of you who is not bidden to come now, and take of the waters of redemption, and drink, and never thirst again.

There are some of you, perhaps, to whom every invitation of Christ's will be made in vain; and that because you have stoutly resolved not to elevate Him to the throne of your hearts. But who these are I know not; and none that are human can tell. Therefore it is that I throw the invitation broadcast among you all, and assure you every one, on the authority of our Lord Himself, that if you will look to Him in penitence and faith, you shall most certainly be saved. If you think otherwise, you question the Redeemer's truthfulness, and pour contempt upon His tears. How can you doubt His sincerity, when you call to mind what He has already done for you, and what He is doing now, to make you know the things which pertain to your peace? Think how often He has visited you with the stingings of conscience, and by the pleadings of the Holy Ghost. Think how He has surrounded you with the means of grace, and has urged you by a thousand considerations to turn from your iniquity and escape the death that never dies. How often has He spoken to you by unexpected mercies, and by unlooked-for afflictions; and how often has He spoken to you in prosperity, and in adversity! Amid joy He has called you; and He has called you amid grief. And you can not say that you did not hear the voice of His invitation. You *did* hear it : you heard it often, you heard it always ; but you have never returned it an answer. The Saviour has dealt honestly and sincerely with you, as you are obliged to admit; and, therefore, if you are not this moment at peace with Him, it is only because you have not accepted His offer of pardon, and have kept far away from Him in heart and in life.

Would that I knew how to make you believe that the exalted Jesus of Nazareth is even now longing to have you come and confess Him as your Redeemer and your eternal Friend; and that while He stands weeping over you, as it were, on the golden steps of His throne, He is stretching forth to you amid His tears the arms of His forgiving love. Oh that you might be made so to feel this that you will never forget it, but let it be to you from this time forth a fountain of out-streaming joy! You ought to feel it, and you ought to believe it; for Christ has done more than enough to prove to you that all of it is true. Think of Him as lamenting over Jerusalem; think of Him as going through Gethsemane's cruel anguish; think of Him as nailed in torture to the cross; think of Him as taking His seat for the sake of His Church upon the right hand of the Father; think of Him as sending the Spirit to convince, and to reprove, and to instruct, all them that formed the travail of His soul,—think of Jesus thus, and doubt no more as to whether He pities you, and is willing to make the light of the knowledge of His glory shine forth in your hearts. He bids you, one and all, to repent, and He bids you to believe. Wherefore, if you will hear His voice, obey Him now, and be reconciled to God. Cast away your jealousy and your suspicions, and earnestly seek Him who says unto you in sincerity, "Look unto Me, all ye ends of the earth, and be ye saved!"

The tears that were shed by Christ over Jerusalem, while they show how honest He is in His offer of salvation, and how anxious He is that all men should avail themselves of it, manifest also the dreadfulness of the doom of them who reject to the last His proffer of pardon and bliss. That must be a dire woe indeed which made the Son of God to weep; and it tells you more plainly than words can tell how unspeakably awful is the loss of the soul. The curse of the Lord of hosts is a hot and withering curse which burns, and burns, for ever. Now this is the malediction that rests upon every one of you who is not a true-hearted disciple of the Saviour's, and is living without God in the world.

If I am now addressing one who is neglecting the stupendous interests of Eternity, I would ask you to remember the foreboding tears of Jesus, and to ponder the fate of those for whom they were shed. I want to know whether you are willing to have wept over you the bitter tears of unavailing regret? I am sure you are not. And yet you are pursuing the same course as those whom the Saviour, even while He wept, consigned without mercy to their unrelenting fate. Beware lest you also have it said of you that the things which have to do with your peace are hid from your eyes. You are holding out in your rebellion against Him who is your rightful King; you are despising His instructions; you are disregarding His entreaties; and you are stiffening your neck against His mild reproofs and against the tender invitations of His love. Now, where can all this land you but in the den of despair? Your means of resistance to Christ are growing stronger every day, while the means which He uses to conquer your obstinacy are becoming less and less effectual; so that it is too painfully evident that you are rapidly nearing the time when the Spirit of Jesus will strive with you no more, and when the doom of Jerusalem's inhabitants will settle down in everlasting horror upon your soul.

Alas! I fear me that I perceive the root of your delusion. You think that the Saviour will yet plead with you, and His Spirit yet move upon you, more strongly than ever before; and you hope that you will still be converted in despite of your continued and increasing dislike of the holiness which God requires. But what ground have you for this expectation? You have none whatever. As to the mere question of power, Jesus might have compelled His countrymen to believe in Him by an influence which they could not resist, and thus have saved them from a wretched condemnation. Such, however, was by no means His pleasure; for this could He not have done without violating one of the fundamental principles of His Father's moral government. The people whose destruction He lamented had heard enough, and seen enough, and felt enough, to constrain them to accept Him as their Saviour; but they were unwilling to be constrained, and therefore they were justly given over to an eternal abandonment. Jesus knew that after they had put away from them, as they had, every argument and every admonition, even His omnipotence must not interpose in their behalf; and hence we see Him weeping with sorrow over their coming downfall, which, as a righteous and unchanging God, He could not and would not avert.

Precisely so will Jesus deal with you. You know now that He is solicitous for your spiritual welfare; and you know that He is urging you by

His calls of tenderness to consider without delay the things which belong to your peace. This very moment He comes and promises you eternal life upon the simple and sole condition that you render Him your heart. But He does not tell you that He will proclaim to you the same terms again, or that, should He do it, you will be at all likely to give Him as favorable a hearing as now. How can you venture to defer to the uncertain future the proper consideration of those things which have to do with the welfare of your soul? The future will come; but you may then be lying in your grave. The future will come; but you may then find it impossible,—being racked by pain, or wandering in delirium, or struck with insensibility,—to consider the call which invites you to fellowship with God and Christ. The future will come; but you may then be kept from hearing the beseechings of grace. The future will come; but you may then be so hardened by your continued unbelief that the offer of mercy will fall unheeded on your ears, and your soul can be moved to contrition no more.

Trust not to the future; for the future may work your ruin. Put not off to the morrow that which may be, and ought to be, done to-day. To-day, if you will hear His voice, harden not your heart.

Repent and believe *now*,—while yet you hear the call of mercy, and the gates of Heaven still stand wide. Flee to the Saviour *now*,—before the coming of that time when you may be banished to the land of everlasting gloom. Oh, remember!

> " In that lone land of deep despair
> No Sabbath's heavenly light shall rise ;
> No God regard your bitter prayer,
> No Saviour call you to the skies."

Neglect not the opportunity now given you to make your peace with God. It is this present " now" which is your " accepted time"; and it is this present " now" which is your " day of salvation." To-morrow the things that pertain to your happiness may be hidden from your eyes : to-day you see them, and are moved by them, and feel that you ought to give them instant attention. Accept, then, at once the offer of the Redeemer. Oh, accept it! lest, grieved by your long perverseness, He uplift over you the last tearful wail of regret, and leave you eternally alone.

The Tears of Compassion.

The Sinner's Unjust Suspicions of the Saviour—Christ's Conduct Proves His Sincerity—The Redemption He Wrought Evidence of His Earnest Compassion—The Sufferings He Underwent for Men Guilty and Condemned—No Stronger Proof of His Sincerity Possible—The Love Displayed in this Work of Redemption—The Saviour Warning by His Tears respecting the Things of Man's Peace—Man Disbelieving and Resisting the Admonition—Danger of Salvation's being Hidden from the Sinner's Eyes—The Day of Mercy Now, but Soon the Night of Despair—The Redeemer would Save, and still Invites by His Spirit—Impenitent Man yet Doubting—Offer of Mercy made to the Most Guilty—The Offer Made to all Classes—The Clemency of the Redeemer Still in Operation—Last Call to Attend to the Things Pertaining to Peace.

The Compassionate Tears of Christ.

It may seem to you a very simple proposition, and a proposition which will at once be generally accepted, that the Saviour evinced, by His weeping on Olivet, a sincere desire for the transgressor against Heaven to turn from his evil ways, and live. You assent without hesitation to this announcement; and you think it impossible that any man who receives the Scriptures as divine can refuse the teaching his instant belief. In spite of this admission of yours, however, there is nothing more demonstrably true than the fact that, if you be not a penitent believer in Christ, you have no Bible faith in this Bible representation. Notwithstanding your verbal admissions, you are still suspicious of the Redeemer in your heart; and you can not realize to yourself that He truly loves you, and would make you a co-heir of His kingdom. There is a fear of Him within you,—a distinctly felt doubt of His assurances, even if you can not, or will not, give that doubt expression. The preacher may bring you face to face with Jesus, and may tell you, and even cause you to feel to some extent, that He is longing to admit you to His embrace; yet will you not lay hold of the declaration and be glad in it with exceeding joy. In a word, you will not really believe it. You may weep, as you hear the Saviour's goodness spoken of; and you may experience a thrill of sensibility in every fibre of your frame, when there is depicted before you the tenderness of His love; but you will still be conscious in your inmost soul that your distrust of Him is not wholly done away, and that He has not become to you a reconciled Friend. You will not "know" the things that belong to your peace, so as to walk continually in the light of the Redeemer's countenance, and to be comforted by His smiles.

I think that the experience of some of you who read these pages will fall in with this representation; and it will compel you to admit that, however you may have received the proposition in an intellectual point of view, you have never vividly realized it in your heart,—that Jesus is not only unwilling to see you lost, but longs to see you saved. You can not fail to perceive that, did you regard Him as so tender in His affection, and as exercising that affection distinctly and personally towards *you*, you would be sure to find your rest and your satisfaction in returning His love and in obeying His will. Now, you are well aware that you entertain no such regard, and are moved by no such spirit of obedience. You know that, whatever peace you have, and whatever joy, it is not " the peace which passeth all understanding," and not " the joy that is unspeakable and full of glory." The even flow of your lives (if it *is* even), springs from your gratification with the things of earth, and has not its source in the contentment which the Redeemer bestows. You are reposing in quiet, and are little disturbed by anxiety (if this *is* in truth your condition), not because you think Him to be your Friend, but because you manage to keep Him out of your thoughts, and to forget that you have an account to render Him as a Saviour that has been doubted, and a Saviour that has been despised.

It is my desire to convince you at present, not that this distrust of a kind and merciful Redeemer is a thing of guilt,—which indeed it is,—but that there is absolutely no reason for it at all. I want to show you, by the Spirit's aid, that there is nothing to hinder you, save your own self-imposed blindness, from seeing the face of Jesus shining upon you from out the darkness; and that there is nothing to prevent you, except your own unworthy and injurious suspicions, from believing in your soul that He is casting on you a look of kindly regard, and holding forth to you the arms of His beseeching love.

I take it for granted that you are prepared to admit that, whatever be your natural and acquired virtues and accomplishments, you are, if unrenewed in heart, both in your feelings and in your practices, forgetters of the Saviour,—living without Him in the world as well in thought as in affection; and I suppose that, knowing yourselves to be in this condition, you believe those representations of the Scripture which declare that condemnation rests upon you, and that, notwithstanding all that may be amiable, and praiseworthy, and fascinating, in your character, you are what the apostle calls "vessels of wrath fitted for destruction." I presume that you accept the Bible doctrine that, if the love of Christ is not in you, you are "dead in trespasses and sins," and are, therefore, no less than the vilest, subjects of the stern malediction of an outraged Law.

Believing this representation, you will perceive that, if the Redeemer has done that which will reinstate you in God's favor, and free you from the curse of the Law, He has given a clear proof of His interest in your behalf and of His wish to save you from ruin. Now, He *has* afforded you just such evidence of His desire for your welfare; and He appeals to it this day as His solemn assurance that He is anxious to clasp every one of you who is still unpardoned to His forgiving breast. Suppose He had left you to yourselves: suppose He had declined to execute the plan of salvation which He and the Father devised; suppose He had not broken down the barrier which Sin had raised between Jehovah and a guilty world; suppose He had not thrust aside with His own hands the obstacles that interposed betwixt the Creator and His offending creatures; suppose He had not made an atonement for iniquity by taking the burden of it upon Himself, and brought in an everlasting righteousness by His perfect obedience, and borne in His own body the chastisement of your peace: suppose, I say, that Jesus of Nazareth had not carried out this mighty scheme of redemption, what else would you have been,—yes, every one of you, —but the eternal prey of your evil passions and

7*

eternal outcasts from the presence of the Lord and from the glory of His power? Had Jesus desired your death, He needed only to leave you to your own course; and His aim would have been reached. Had He wished you to be ruined, it was only necessary for Him to let the poison of sin work within you; and tell you of no remedy. But, He did not want you to perish; He did not want you to be swept off in your guilt to the pit of the lost. Oh, no; it is not this that Jesus has ever desired. He has desired rather to save you from your sins, and to constitute you the inheritors of unending bliss. He wants to transform you from "vessels of wrath" into "vessels of mercy"; He wants to change you from enemies to friends; He wants to turn you from the paths of disobedience into the paths of righteousness; He wants to bring you to Himself as loving brethren, and to exhibit you as the monuments of His pardoning grace.

If you doubt these assertions, consider what the Saviour has done in the work of redemption to make you the partakers of heavenly joy. "In bondage under the elements of the world", both by nature and by practice, you have been rescued from your slavery by His crucifixion, and you have made to you the offer of reconciliation with an ill-treated and offended Sovereign. Yes, Jesus of Nazareth, the only-begotten of the Father, took upon Himself the curse of the Law for your sake; and for your sake He fulfilled that Law to its uttermost requirement. There was none in all the universe that could have done this except the spotless Lamb of God. He has died for you, to free you from the malediction which rests upon your souls; and He has gone up into Heaven for you, to be unto you the Mediator of the new and everlasting covenant, and that He may show forth in you the abundant riches of His favor. Not content with putting into your hand a certificate of acquittal from your guilt, He is bent on giving you a title-deed to a mansion in His celestial home. Not satisfied with wiping off from you the taint of rebellion, He is determined to clothe you in the robes of heavenly priests and kings, and to secure for you all the blessings which result from "the adoption of sons".

Sure am I that these are wondrous things which the Redeemer, even your Redeemer, has done in your behalf; and it is impossible for you really to believe that He has effected all this for your sake, and yet to doubt His sincerity when He laments over your blindness to the things of your welfare.

Consider the nature of His wrought-out salvation; and observe how He proves that He means what He says when He asks you to turn to Him and live. Note how wonderful, and how undeserved, is this kindness of the Saviour. Think how, though you are guilty, and alienated from Him in heart and life, He offers you pardon; and not only pardon, but redemption; and not only redemption, but justification; and not only justification, but adoption,—and this adoption an inheritance among the saints in light. Look over these blessings,—held out to you, all of them, as the gifts of Jesus' grace,—reflect on their magnitude; and then doubt, if you can, that He is altogether in earnest, when He says to each of you, "Oh that thou wouldst know, even thou, at least in this thy day, the things which belong unto thy peace!"

If what the Redeemer has done in the working out of man's salvation does not show that He is desirous to rescue the sinful from destruction, there is no truth whatever that is capable of proof. A stupendous undertaking was it indeed even for Him, to attempt to procure the sinner's justification. The difficulty which had to be met was a difficulty which not only man, but the highest archangel, was unable to resolve. The question was, How can the Lawgiver be just, and yet justify those who had broken the Law? The question was, How could the race that had violated the injunctions laid on them in the hearing of the universe be relieved from condemnation, and yet God's character remain untarnished, and the pillars of His government remain unshaken? The question was, How could the Lord be merciful, and yet continue firm to His word and uphold His truthfulness before the eyes of all His intelligent creation? And this was a question to which none among the hosts of Heaven could give a response. They saw the mighty obstacle in the way of the sinner's redemption; and they felt it to be an obstacle which they were not able to remove. They could not imagine how God might pardon the violators of His commandments, and still preserve His honor and His authority among the creatures He had made. They knew not how to magnify the Law, and, even while magnifying it, to redeem the transgressor from its curse; and they knew not how to execute the threatened punishment, and, even while executing it, to lift the penalty from off the shoulders of guilty men.

But, blessed be our Lord and Saviour Jesus Christ, what angels knew not, He knew, and what angels shrunk from undertaking, He undertook, and carried into perfect accomplishment. There came up One from Edom, "travelling in the greatness of his strength"; and there came up One from Bozrah, who was "mighty to save". He it was,— Jesus of Nazareth, the mourner on Olivet,—that entered upon the arduous enterprise of rescuing the sinful and the lost, while He magnified the violated Law, and shed new lustre on the attributes of that God who rules the world in righteousness and truth. On Him was laid the iniquity of us all; and by His stripes we were healed. He bore the dreadful load of our guilt; and into His bosom was poured the red wine-cup of Jehovah's wrath, which we had been condemned to drink, and to drink to the lowest dregs.

There is something wonderful in this lofty undertaking,—something which far surpasses our comprehension, and makes us tremble, when we think of it, with a fearful delight. There is in it the very grandeur of love,—love too high to be reached; love too profound to be fathomed; love too vast to be measured; love which neither words can express, nor thoughts conceive. And tell me, O ye that are doubting the Saviour's assurance of His interest in your well-being, tell me wherefore, if

He does not desire you to be happy for ever, did He pass a life of suffering for you, and die for you in agony upon the cross? Wherefore, if He is not shocked at the thought of your destruction, the sorrows which He heaped upon His own head; wherefore His sad pilgrimage as a man among men; wherefore His cruel privations; and, above all, wherefore His distressing death? There is no argument so potent in proof of His mercy toward the impenitent, as the terrible anguish which He took upon Himself when He endured the storm of God's fury in the transgressor's stead. Oh, His love is a sincere, and all-embracing, and everlasting, love! I see it in the heart-sweat of the garden; I see it in the torturings of the cross; I see it in the hidings of the Father's countenance in that dark hour when the Saviour seemed to be forsaken, and when awful desolateness and sore travail came upon His soul. Herein I read the evidence of Jesus' love to sinners,—to all sinners, even to you; and I hear Him saying in tones of tenderness such as He alone can use, " Oh that ye would know, even ye, at least in this your day, the things which belong unto your peace!"

Yes, ye impenitent and unbelieving, there are things that belong to your peace; and there is a day in which it becomes you to attend to them, lest they be wholly and for ever hid from your eyes. The Saviour is anxious in your behalf; fearing that you will continue to neglect the matters which pertain to your salvation, until it is too late to think of them, and you are left without Christ and without hope. Take warning, I beseech you, from His tears of compassion shed over Jerusalem; and look upon these tears as one of the strongest proofs He has ever given of His unwillingness that any should perish, and of His desire for all to come to Him as their Redeemer, and find eternal life.

You have been taught in various ways what those things are which pertain to your salvation; and the Redeemer would now by His Spirit bring them again to your remembrance. He reminds you of your enmity to God and your long disobedience to His will,—declaring that for this you must repent from the heart, and resolve to forsake all your sins. He reminds you, furthermore, that, while repentance is good, and proper, and even rigidly demanded; yet that the sincerest repentance is of no avail, unless it is accompanied by faith in the Lord Jesus Christ. This faith He exhorts you to acquire,—telling you that it is the turning-point of your acceptance with God. He assures you that, though you are sinful, and, as such, obnoxious to punishment, yet He has made ample provision for your justification before the Father, and for your growth in holiness until you become meet for Heaven. To believe that He has done this, to believe it in the soul, is faith,—that faith which He commands you to seek, if you would truly know the things which belong to your peace. The Redeemer offers you a perfect salvation; and there is nothing to prevent you from securing it except your want of faith. Oh, struggle to attain the faith required, —imploring God to give it to you; for the lack of it is due to the rooted unwillingness of your minds to believe that Jesus loves you, and would save you from destruction. Do battle with this fixed perverseness of your hearts; strive to realize the goodness of Christ; and seek to lay hold of Him as your righteousness and your strength, in a firm reliance upon the efficacy of His death and the power of His mediation.

I know not how long each of you has been resisting the Saviour's entreaty that you should attend to the things which belong to your peace; but I do know that there is no one of you, unrepentant and unbelieving to-day, who is not in danger of having all these things hidden from his eyes. With some of you Jesus has borne very many years; and, though a thousand times He has been about to desert you, a thousand times He has refrained. Others of you have had a shorter period of probation; but, warned few times or many times, you are drawing nearer and nearer to that hour when you shall be warned no more. All of you are under sentence of condemnation; and you have been spared so far to prove to you, and to all the universe, that the Redeemer takes no pleasure in your ruin. You are indebted to His long-suffering more, perhaps, than you suppose. Not only has He extended the period of your reprieve again and again; but He has plied you meanwhile with all the agencies of salvation,—urging them upon you with a pertinacity that would not be denied; and has striven most earnestly to lead you to repentance and to the obedience which springs from faith.

I would remind you, as I array these facts before your mental vision, that you, on your part, have done, and are now doing, all you can to frustrate the kind intentions of the Saviour. You are putting away from you every offer of mercy,—thus riveting more tightly the chains of your condemnation. Why will you not remember that, though Jesus wishes all men to know the things which pertain to their salvation, yet millions upon millions have had them hidden from their eyes? The Redeemer desires you to be saved; but that is very far from saying you will be saved. To be frank with you, there are some among you who give your Christian acquaintances little reason to hope that you will ever find the path of life. The offer of pardon and of a blissful eternity has often been made to you, and made sincerely; but you have as often rejected it, and have gone on increasing in impenitence and obduracy of heart. Yes, the Saviour has favored you indeed; but you are still barren fig-trees in His vineyard, and He is getting ready to cut you down. Think of the days, and the months, and the years, which have been granted you for spiritual improvement; call to mind the privileges of many a sweet Sabbath; recollect the entreaties of ministers and of friends; remember your Heaven-sent comforts and Heaven-sent afflictions; and then consider how you have let all these means of grace pass by unappropriated, and have not regarded the things which belong to your peace. You can not deny that Jesus has been very indulgent to you in giving you so favorable a day of probation; and you can not deny that He would be just, were He now to withdraw all His gracious influences and leave you to your doom. And how do you know that He is not about to forsake you, and call you by His Gospel never again? You have not believed Him; you have not obeyed Him; and verily He would deal with you righteously, were He now to depart from you, and never more present to you the offer of salvation.

This is the day of your acceptance, O ye impenitent,—a day of Gospel teaching, a day of precious privileges, a day of grand opportunities; but a day which will soon be followed by a night that has no end. The time is short: therefore, what you have to do, do it quickly and with all your strength. Every moment you now lose is more precious than gold; for each minute that flits along towards eternity bears with it some portion of the life-blood of your souls. Soon you will pass the point beyond which it is impossible to retrace your steps; and then you will be utterly undone. To-day you may know the things which belong to your peace: to-morrow,—the sad to-morrow in which the Saviour ceases to plead, and only weeps,—all these things will be hid from your eyes. You see now: but beware lest blindness come upon you,—that blindness which not even a sunbeam from Heaven can remove, that blindness for which there is no compensation, that blindness which consigns the soul to a darkness that may be felt amid the regions where hope and mercy are unknown.

I desire to have you distinctly understand that the Redeemer is now extending to you each another invitation to be reconciled to the Father through faith in the Son. His messenger comes and assures you, upon evidence which you ought not to doubt, that Jesus will be delighted to see you attending to the things that have to do with your eternal destiny. To you each is this word of exhortation personally addressed; and you are called on, every one of you, to listen to the voice that speaks to you from Heaven, and to open to the Saviour who is knocking at the door of your hearts. Oh, I do believe that the Spirit of the living God is now at work upon you; and I am sure that, if you will suffer Him, He will give energy to what has been said, and convert your souls. Turn not away from Him; steel not your breasts against Him,—lest you lose the knowledge which He alone can impart. The Spirit can make you behold what now is dark, if you will ask Him for light. The Spirit can reveal to you the enormity of your guilt, if you will pray for a deeper conviction. The Spirit can make you believe, if you will beg Him to give you faith. The Spirit can melt down your stubbornness, if you will humbly and penitently submit yourselves to the workings of His power. The Spirit can make you perceive the value of salvation, and can enable you to lay hold on eternal life. The Spirit can cause the rays of a divine illumination to break forth within you, and make you see "the light of the knowledge of God's glory in the face of Jesus Christ." Pray, then, earnestly for the Spirit's aid; that what has been spoken to you about the compassion of Christ may be blest to your conversion, and that your bosoms may be made to palpitate this day with the throbbings of a new-born faith.

In spite of all that has been said, some of you still entertain ungenerous suspicions of the Redeemer, and you will not really believe that He desires to save you, and render you the trophies of His grace. But, I assure you, it is true, and very true, that He is even now striving to bring you to Himself,—that your fellowship may henceforth be with the Father and with the Son. He is even now begging you to cast aside your fears, and to put your hand upon the covenant of redemption.

Will you not listen to the warm pleadings of His voice, as He says to you, "Oh that ye would know, even ye, at least in this your day, the things which belong unto your peace!" Mark you, there is no threatening here. There is nothing but the beseeching tenderness of love. And I do think that, when Jesus thus condescends to entreat you, when He woos you by sweet solicitations, when He pours out before you the fullness of His fraternal heart, you ought to hear Him, and you ought to turn to Him, and you ought to obey His call.

Some of you are still afraid of the Saviour; for you feel that you are awfully guilty in His sight. But why should you shrink back from the Redeemer who tells you that, if you will trust in Him, it matters not though your sins be as scarlet, they shall be white as snow? Why should you stay away from Him, when He says to you that He is waiting to be gracious, and that He is ready to press you to His bosom as the brethren of his love? By His long-suffering and goodness, by His tears shed upon Olivet, by His solemn declarations, I do protest to you that you are wronging Him as a tender-hearted Saviour; and doing despite to the invitations of His grace. Your fears are wholly without foundation. Seek Him with full purpose of soul; and you shall find Him, and shall rejoice in Him with abounding joy. Cease from your unkind doubts, and throw yourselves into the arms of His mercy. Believe that He grieves over your determination to perish; believe that He wishes you to live, and that therefore He has suffered for you, and died for you, and risen for you from the grave, and ascended for you to His mediatorial throne. Believe this, believe it in your hearts; and salvation will have come to you from above.

I want to remind you again, before I conclude, that the offer of the Saviour's mercy is now made to you all without exception.. It matters not whether you be such as have fallen from your first love, and come afresh under condemnation; or whether you be such as are just beginning to be anxious about the interests of your souls, and have learned that God has a controversy with you; or whether you be such as are to a great extent indifferent to the kindness of your Redeemer, but yet are troubled at times in view of the future; or whether you be such as care not at all for the claims of God and the claims of Christ,—to one and all of you the Saviour says, in a voice of tenderness that ought to melt the coldest heart, "Oh, that ye might know, even ye, at least in this your day, the things which belong to your peace!" There is not one among you to whom He does not now hold out the promise of pardon, if you will repent of your sins, and seek Him in the manner of His appointment. I care not how wicked you are, the Redeemer is not willing that you should die, but greatly prefers that you should live. You may have gone very far away from your Heavenly Father, and have sinned against Him with a high hand, and have forsaken the covenant made with Him in former years, and have crucified afresh your Lord and Saviour Jesus Christ; but, notwithstanding all, the Redeemer does not want to see you perish, but wants to make you the co-heirs of His kingdom and the possessors of perfect peace.

Some of you have long lived for every thing else but Christ; but even you He is unwilling to leave to your merited fate. Seek Him, then, in this your day; seek Him before the night of death draws nigh, and before the time of mercy is over; and ask Him to speak the words of forgiveness to your souls. Your childhood is gone; your youth is gone; your riper years are gone; and now you are in the sere and yellow leaf of advancing age. There is, however, a little hope for you yet. Oh, lay hold upon it, lest it vanish away and leave you to darkness and despair!

The sins of some of you are aggravated; for they have been against light and knowledge such as, if given even in a tithe of it to others, would have led them to salvation. But as for you, you have abused your privileges, and despised your advantages, until you have run up against you I know not how tremendous an account of guilt. Yet, for you also there is pardon; for it is even over you,—yea, the very worst of you,—that Jesus lifts up the voice of His beseechings, and begs you to attend to the things which belong to your peace while the Gospel day still shines upon you, and the night of evil has not come.

I know not the precise spiritual condition of any of you whom I now address; but I do know that there is no one among you to whom the Redeemer is not this moment extending the hands of His clemency, and imploring you to seek His face while yet He may be found. There is nothing between you and a Saviour ready to receive you but your obstinate unbelief. You are not straitened in Him; but are straitened in yourselves, and in yourselves alone. You need not say, any one of you, that you are too great a sinner to be accepted; for it was sinners whom Jesus came to call to His kingdom and glory. You need not say that you are too utterly lost ever to be rescued; for Jesus came to seek and to save that which is lost. It is enough, if you feel your wickedness, and will forsake it. This will deliver you from death. It is enough, if you know that you are wanderers from the Saviour, and are resolved to return to Him. He will receive you, and make you His friends.

Look unto the Redeemer, every one of you, and rejoice in His abounding love. As an ambassador for Christ, I do beseech you to be reconciled to Him whom you have so grossly offended. He is willing, nay, He is anxious, for you all to become the subjects of His forgiving grace. Would that I knew how to lead you to believe this; and would that I could make you feel that it is *you* whom Jesus calls in person, and *you* whom He warns in person, when He says, "Oh that ye might know, even ye, at least in this your day, the things which belong unto your peace!" Now, it *is* you to whom He speaks; and it is *you* for whose salvation He fears; and it is *you* to whom He says, in addition, "Come unto Me, and I will in no wise cast you out." Wherefore, hear His invitation, and give heed to it, that you may not have the things of your peace for ever hidden from your eyes. Seize fast upon the Saviour's promise; and begin from this hour to exercise the faith, and to put forth the obedience, of those who have been called out of nature's darkness into the Gospel's marvellous light.

www.ingramcontent.com/pod-product-compliance
Lightning Source LLC
Chambersburg PA
CBHW031453160426
43195CB00010BB/964